MW00872714

PRO AI PROMPT PUBLISHING

AI Image Prompts

Over 500 Stable Diffusion and Midjourney Prompts

Copyright © 2023 by Pro AI Prompt Publishing

All rights reserved. No part of this publication may be reproduced, stored or transmitted in any form or by any means, electronic, mechanical, photocopying, recording, scanning, or otherwise without written permission from the publisher. It is illegal to copy this book, post it to a website, or distribute it by any other means without permission.

First edition

Contents

Introduction

This book features over 500 professionally engineered Stable Diffusion and Midjourney prompts. Simply type the prompts into the AI image generators and watch your amazing artistic creations come to life. Below is a brief overview for using the various AI engines.

Stable Diffusion

There are many ways to use the Stable Diffusion engine. You can download and run on your own computer, or you can use the following options in any web browser.

- NightCafe (https://nightcafe.studio/)
- Clipdrop (https://clipdrop.co/)
- DreamStudio (https://dreamstudio.ai/)

Simply sign up, then type your prompt and click generate.

Midjourney

- To use Midjourney you must first sign up for an account at (https://www.midjourney.com/)
- Currently Midjourney is only available for use through discord, but you can download the app and sign up here (https://discord.com/)
- Then follow the steps to get started using the quick start guide (https://docs.midjourney.com/docs/quick-start)

Happy generating!

Stable Diffusion

Beautiful Women

did you know, that when my eyes become large and the light that you shine can be seen, I might compare you to a kiss from a dionaea muscipula, trending on artstation, sharp focus, studio photo, intricate details, highly detailed, by greg rutkowski

A smiling Asian woman poses for the camera with an oshare kei flair, showcasing intricate details in light gray and light brown tones. The composition features tightly framed scenes with a soft yet lively touch, exuding a gentle and vibrant atmosphere.

A detailed, abstract portrait of a stunning young Scottish woman, captured in 8K HDR with cinematic lighting. Enhanced by ray tracing, she is set against a starry universe backdrop, creating a dramatic and immersive atmosphere.

the real close-up of beautiful young Scottish girl, extremely detailed texture, Rendered in 8K HDR with cinematic lighting, dramatic atmosphere, Enhanced by ray tracing, set against a starry universe backdrop for added depth.

An astonishing photo of a young woman from Panama: detailed, realistic, and captivating. The portrait showcases delicate skin nuances, expressive facial elements. Full Body, The high-detail RAW color art captures her allure and intensity. Shot in muted soft lighting with a shallow depth of focus, her evocative posture and penetrating gaze are in sharp focus. The result is an incredibly lifelike, cinematic, work of art.

Beautiful Brazilian woman with porcelain, flawless skin, and ethereal beauty. Beautiful eyes, dark and deep, are accentuated by eyeliner; arched eyebrows and softy lips add tenderness. Silk kimonos and ornate hairpieces enhance her enchanting visage. Captured in a RAW portrait through professional photography, high resolution,32k.

A warm, impressionistic painting of a super cute woman smiling gently, her big reflective eyes focused on a dancing flame of a candle she holds. "

a beautiful young hot, lusty, steamy Brazilian woman on a hot summer day in Havana. Panoramic shot with wide-angle lens showcases their beauty and casual poses amidst colorful architecture, vintage cars, and steamy streets. sweaty skin, extreme hot summer day, washed ripped jeans

The image features a beautiful young woman posing in front of a military vehicle, likely a tank. She is wearing a green shirt and a brown vest, and her long blonde hair. The woman is smiling and appears to be enjoying her time in the presence of the military vehicle. portrait photography, dynamic composition, masterpiece, highly detail. 35mm photograph, film, bokeh, professional, 4k, highly detailed.

The image features a beautiful young woman wearing a black dress. She is posing for the camera, with her hands on her hips, showcasing her confidence and style. The woman is standing in front of a white background, which emphasizes her as the main subject of the photo. The black dress she is wearing is elegant and stylish, complementing her overall appearance.

The image features a beautiful ((freckles)) girl wearing a black dress, standing in a dimly lit room. She is looking down, simply enjoying the ambiance. The woman is adorned with a necklace, adding to her elegant appearance. The room appears to be a living space, with a couch visible in the background. The overall atmosphere of the scene is sophisticated and intimate.

The image features a woman wearing lipstick, a black hat and a tosca ribbon around her top dress. She is posing for the camera, and her face is partially covered by the hat. The woman appears to be wearing a black dress, which complements her overall appearance. The scene is set against a black and white background, adding a touch of elegance to the image.

The image features a woman standing in the beach, small waves, highly detailed, HRD CLoud, extreme weather with a beautiful sunset in the background. She is wearing a flowing dress, which adds to the serene and picturesque atmosphere of the scene. The woman appears to be walking or standing still in the water, enjoying the tranquility and beauty of the moment. The sunset casts a warm glow on the water, enhancing the overall ambiance of the scene.

The image features a young girl sitting on a chair, full of laughter, wearing a white blouse and a red skirt. She is posing for a portrait, and her expression is focused. The woman is sitting on a wooden chair, which adds a natural and rustic touch to the scene. The overall atmosphere of the picture is calm and intimate, with the woman's attire and the wooden chair creating a warm and inviting ambiance.

masterpiece, a stunning full body portrait of a gorgeous lady named Isabella, wearing a minimum transparent and translucent outfit, exuding sultry elegance. The setting is a ballroom, detailed, cinematic, and hyperrealistic. The portrait reflects a photo-realistic quality and an expressive art style, formatted in a 9:16 aspect ratio

The image features a woman wearing a blue hat and a blue dress, holding a glass filled with a green liquid, possibly a cocktail. She is also wearing a ring and a necklace, adding to her elegant appearance. The woman is standing in front of a lime, which is a key ingredient in the cocktail she is holding. The scene captures a stylish and sophisticated atmosphere, with the woman enjoying her drink and showcasing her fashionable attire.

The image features a beautiful woman with long, curly hair, posing for a portrait. She is wearing a tosca shirt and has her hair styled in loose, flowing waves. Her facial expression is captivating, with her eyes closed and her lips slightly parted, creating a sense of tranquility and serenity. The woman is standing in front of a plain background, which allows the focus to be solely on her appearance and the artistic composition of the portrait.

Masterpiece RAW photo: Portrait of a stylish woman beside a city high-rise window, short wavy hair, elegant white lace evening gown, 50mm f/1.4 lens, high detail, sharp focus, dramatic rim light, cowboy shot, sunset, 8K UHD.

The image features a beautiful Romanian young woman with long, dark hair, wearing a white shirt and white shorts, She is standing on a street, posing for the camera with a smile on her face. The woman's outfit is casual and comfortable, making her look stylish and confident. The scene captures a moment of her daily life, showcasing her unique sense of fashion and style.

(masterpiece, RAW photo), portrait photo of a trendy beautiful girl from Belarus, short wavy hair, beautiful white evening dress, lace, intricate, , 50mm, f/1. 4, high detail, sharp focus, cowboy shot, rim light, sunset, 8K UHD

The image features a Spanish beautiful woman wearing a white dress and a white hat, sitting at a dining table. She is posing for the camera, and her outfit is complemented by a pearl necklace. The table has a cup and a vase on it, adding to the elegant atmosphere of the scene. The woman appears to be enjoying her time, social setting.

An image of a woman with flowing, dark hair dons a white shirt and appears lost in thought or perhaps in a state of relaxation. Her gaze is directed downward, her eyes possibly closed, as her hair dances in the wind, imbuing the scene with a sense of dynamism. The ambiance is one of tranquil serenity, capturing the woman in a moment of pure enjoyment.

RAW photo, photo of a young Spanish girl, on a New York City rooftop, high-fashion editorial, urban backdrop, real photo, fashion shot, rooftop fashion, 85mm prime lens, confident supermodel, skyline view, modern elegance.

Gorgeous lady in a sheer black coat, captured in full-body pose with closed eyes. The image is a result of a high-quality photoshoot, featuring symmetry and incredible detail at an 8k resolution. The photograph is a photorealistic masterpiece created through professional photography with the use of natural lighting. The composition is maximalist and intricately detailed, resembling concept art with its complexity and maximum attention to details.

The image features a beautiful woman wearing a red hat with a feather, a black dress, and a pair of earrings. She is posing for a picture, and her outfit is complemented by a red lipstick on her lips. The woman's attire and the feather in her hat give her a stylish and elegant appearance.

A cheerful, confident and stylish young Italian girl poses on a sunlit sidewalk, captured in a high-detail RAW color photograph. She's wear no make-up, light red lipstik, has Natural Frickes skin complexion, dressed in a white shirt and blue jeans, perfectly accented by a pair of high heels. The sunlight illuminates her, emphasizing her fashionable attire and radiant presence. The composition captures her in a dynamic pose, making her the focal point while subtly highlighting the urban setting around her.

The image features a woman wearing a white hat and a white dress, standing in front of a building. She is holding a cup, possibly a coffee mug, in her hand. The woman appears to be posing for a picture, and there is a chair visible in the background. The scene captures a moment of elegance and style, with the woman's outfit and accessories complementing her overall appearance.

Gorgeous model strutting the runway at a fashion show, wearing breathtaking summer outfits with intricate batik pattern details. The outdoor view near the beach highlights every smallest detail, making the catwalk come alive.

A cheerful, confident and stylish young Italian girl, hyper-realistic photo, in the style of intricate body-painting, mysterious beauty, uhd image, tattoo

A woman with blonde hair of considerable length stands on the beach, exuding a blend of dark gold and light bronze tones. She wears modern jewelry that shines brilliantly, reminiscent of radiant clusters. The lighting complements her appearance, highlighting a youthful energy. Her style evokes the charm of the French countryside, characterized by distinct and unparalleled pieces.

A lifelike image of a young woman, full of expression, taken using a Fujifilm GFX 100 and a 110mm f/2 lens. The photo captures realism with well-balanced studio lighting, preserving the emotional intensity of her gaze. Shot away from city bustle, against a stormy sky, her intense stare echoing in the dramatic clouds. In 8K resolution with HDR, rich details, RTX technology, cinematic lighting, and Unreal Engine.

The image features a woman standing on a stool, wearing a blue shirt and jeans. She is posing for a picture, and her hair is blowing in the wind. The woman appears to be confident and stylish, showcasing her outfit and the casual yet fashionable vibe of her attire. The stool adds an interesting element to the composition, as it elevates the woman and draws attention to her presence in the scene.

An awe-inspiring photo of a young woman from China: detailed, realistic, and captivating. The portrait showcases intricate skin characteristics, emotive facial traits. Full Body, The high-detail RAW color art captures her magnetism and determination. Shot in soft, diffused light with a limited depth of focus, her captivating stance and penetrating gaze are in sharp focus. The outcome is a hyper-detailed, filmic, masterpiece..

The image features a woman wearing a black hat, a black dress, and a pearl necklace. She is posing for a picture, and her lips are painted red. The woman is also wearing a black glove, which adds to her elegant and stylish appearance. The combination of her outfit, makeup, and accessories creates a sophisticated and timeless look.

a closeup picture of a beautiful young Turkish woman in a traditional Russian Tsar costume, in the style of salon kei, photo-realistic techniques, 32k, uhd, Canon, classical, historical genre scenes, serene face.

front shot, portrait photo of a 23 y.o beautiful cheerful brunette Armenian woman, thin Pinkish glossy lipstik, looks away, natural Frickes skin complexion, skin moles,

The image features a woman standing near a body of water, wearing a dark geen sweater and a necklace. The woman is positioned close to the water, with her sweater and necklace adding a touch of elegance to the scene. The overall atmosphere of the image is serene and captivating, as the woman's presence near the water creates a sense of tranquility and beauty.

The photo showcases a woman who appears to be in her early to mid-twenties. Her complexion is clear and fair, and she has a heart-shaped face, with high cheekbones and a pointed chin. Her eyes are almond-shaped and of a deep brown color, framed by well-defined eyebrows. Her hair, a rich shade of brown, is styled in loose waves that frame her face and extends down to her shoulders. She is wearing a burgundy-colored top, which adds a warm contrast to her light skin tone. Around her neck, she has a simple silver necklace with a small pendant. The woman is looking slightly to her left, away from the camera, and her lips are parted as if she is about to speak or is in the middle

9

of a conversation. Her expression is somewhat reflective, adding an air of mystery to the image. The photo is taken outdoors, as indicated by the natural light that illuminates her face and the blurred greenery in the background. This outdoor setting adds a sense of freshness and vitality to the image. The photo appears to have been professionally taken, with the woman sharply in focus against the blurred background, creating a pleasing depth of field effect.

A cheerful, confident and stylish young Italian girl poses on a sunlit sidewalk, captured in a high-detail RAW color photograph. She's wear no make-up, light red lipstik, has Natural Frickes skin complexion, dressed in a white shirt and blue jeans, perfectly accented by a pair of high heels. The sunlight illuminates her, emphasizing her fashionable attire and radiant presence. The composition captures her in a dynamic pose, making her the focal point while subtly highlighting the urban setting around her.

From below, a portrait of a stunning woman illuminated with accent lighting. The style exudes dynamic and intense emotions, featuring rich cinematic color grading for a photorealistic, 32k-quality look. Captured with a Canon EOS-1D X Mark III, this photorealistic masterpiece by Mark Keathley, a Shutterstock contest winner, resonates with raw emotion. Thom Wasserman's intricate and captivating scene, taken using a Fujifilm GFX 100S medium format mirrorless camera and GF 32-64mm f/4 R LM WR lens at 45mm focal length, embodies exceptional clarity and detail.

The image features a beautiful young woman wearing a red coat and black leather pants. She is standing on a sidewalk, possibly posing for a picture. The woman is holding a handbag, which is placed close to her body. The scene captures her style and confidence as she stands out in the city

Full-bodied modern woman by window, hair flowing, intricate detail, perfect composition, soft evening light, clear eyes and face, rich colors.

The image features a beautiful woman wearing a hat and a dress. She is posing for the camera, looking at it with a smile on her face. The woman's outfit is elegant and stylish, and her smile adds a sense of warmth and charm to the scene. The image captures a moment of confidence and grace, showcasing the woman's beauty and poise.

accent lighting, from below body portrait of stuning beautiful woman as music, wincore, stripcore, In the style of sound, dynamic, intense and raw emotion, rich, cinematic color grading, stunning, photorealistic, 32k, shot on Canon EOS-1D X Mark III, photorealistic painting, by Mark Keathley, Shutterstock contest winner, iPhone,e video, photo taken of an epic intricate, Thom Wasserman, he photograph is taken using a Fujifilm GFX 100S medium format mirrorless camera, paired with the GF 32-64mm f/4 R LM WR lens set at a focal length of 45mm, capturing the captivating scene with exceptional detail and clarity

A very beautiful young woman from France is captured in a detailed 6K portrayal, her captivating smile accentuated by medium lighting that adds depth to her features. The artwork follows the rule of thirds, creating a stunning and atmospheric masterpiece, Perfect Anatomy

Kodak disposable camera, featuring an alluring woman seated in an office, her captivating smile carrying a hint of suggestion. The photo quality is set at a level of 5 out of 5.

the real close-up of beautiful young Scottish girl, extremely detailed texture, Rendered in 8K HDR with cinematic lighting, dramatic atmosphere, Enhanced by ray tracing, set against a starry universe backdrop for added depth.

A breathtaking photo of a young woman from France: detailed, realistic, and captivating. The portrait showcases intricate skin textures, vivid facial attributes. Full Body, The high-detail RAW color art captures her grace and determination. Shot in muted soft light with a shallow depth of focus, her alluring posture and penetrating gaze are in sharp focus. The outcome is an incredibly lifelike, movie-like, masterpiece.

A mesmerizing photo of a young woman from Spain: detailed, realistic, and captivating. The portrait showcases delicate skin details, expressive facial characteristics. Full Body, The high-detail RAW color art captures her allure and determination. Shot in soft, diffused illumination with a limited depth of focus, her captivating stance and intense stare are in sharp focus. The outcome is a hyper-detailed, cinematic, marvel.

"Beautiful cheerfull girl with Romanian features, wearing a dress from the Summer Dress Collection. She has high detail natural complexion skin and green eyes, framed in a dynamic shot. Shallow depth of field, beautiful dramatic lighting."

Photoshoot by fabulous Annie Leibovitz, 60-30-10 color rule, divine proportion, spectacular, in autumn park the Delightfully figure of chess, 32k, divine proportion, ultra detailed textures, perfect proportions, exuding a sense of mysterious allure, epic character, photoshoot in beautifully lit, magic atmosphere

In a surreal dance of delicate movement, the ethereal beauty is captured in this portrait of a midair dancer. The soft pastel tones, backlighting, and flowing fabric create a dreamlike ambiance. The image features cinematic lighting and is presented in ultra-high resolution with an aspect ratio of 9:16

The image features a woman walking down a sidewalk while holding a cup of coffee in her hand. She is wearing a dark gret dress and high heels, giving her a stylish appearance. The woman is also carrying a handbag, which is placed close to her side. In the background, there are a few other people walking on the sidewalk, and a motorcycle is parked nearby. The scene captures a typical day in an urban setting, with people going about their daily routines.

The image features a woman wearing a white hat with a red flower on it. She is also wearing a red lipstick, which complements her outfit. The woman is looking at the camera, and her face is the main focus of the image. The combination of the white hat, red lipstick, and the woman's gaze creates a visually striking and elegant scene.

A young woman from France is captured in a detailed 6K portrayal, her captivating smile accentuated by medium lighting that adds depth to her features. The artwork follows the rule of thirds, creating a stunning and atmospheric masterpiece.

Photoshoot closeup of gorgeous beauty that is hard to imagine Crazy dance at Masquerade Night Ball mandy disher, gloomy villainess in fifth dimension, unbelievable stunning view, splash iridescent light around her, stunning neon grading undertones airy scifi, 32K, divine proportion, cinematic lighting, artificial lighting, hyper detailed, realistic intricate details, sharp focus, hyper realism, detailed character design, sharp focus, stunning art by Henri Cartier Bresson, Annie Leibovitz, Steve McCurry

"An ultra-high-definition 32K photo portrays a woman with blue eyes gazing at her reflection. The image, rendered in hyper-realistic detail, employs a palette of light indigo and dark amber. It draws inspiration from Orientalist style and romantic fantasy, featuring idealized depictions of Native Americans with intense close-up shots.

A beautiful woman style of Agnes Cecile, Frank Bramley, Anne Bachelier

A finely detailed depiction of a stunning Viking warrior woman, illuminated with cinematic lighting, reflections, and ray tracing effects. Created using Octane Render, the artwork is in sharp focus and boasts a seamless 8K resolution. Crafted as a digital painting, it's gaining popularity on ArtStation. Crafted collaboratively by Seb McKinnon and Greg Rutkowski.

A (((captivating))) photo of (((a young woman from France))): detailed, realistic, and captivating. The portrait showcases (((detailed skin features))), (((expressive facial traits))). (((Full Body))), The high-detail RAW color art captures her beauty and intensity. Shot in (((soft diffused glow))) with (((a shallow depth of range))), (((her suggestive posture))) and (((penetrating stare))) are in sharp focus. The result is a (((highly-realistic))), (((cinematic wonder))), (((work))).

A compelling 3K depiction of an Afghan beauty, her eyes filled with intrigue, and the lighting, reminiscent of Quentin Blake's approach, adding a touch of whimsy. The portrait captures her allure and depth in a unique way.

"A beautiful Italian girl, 21 years old, natural complexion skin, with wild dark hair and smokey eye shadow, posing in a dynamic angle under volumetric lighting, captured in Ultra HD.

The image features a beautiful woman wearing a dark tosca dress, sitting on a chair and holding a glass of beer. She appears to be enjoying her drink and is the main focus of the scene. There are several other people in the background, but they are not the main subject of the image. The woman's elegant posture and the beer in her hand create a relaxed and enjoyable atmosphere.

A dancer adorned with feathers and jewelry performs at night on a beach by a fire, inspired by the artistic styles of Magali Villeneuve, Eve Ventrue, and Anna Dittmann. The artwork features a realistic depiction of light using luminous pointillism techniques. Created with Daz3D and influenced by The Stars Art Group (Xing Xing) and Sultan Mohammed, the scene evokes a sense of mystique. The dancer's presence contrasts against a backdrop of stars, capturing a burnt and charred atmosphere.

Yennefer z Vengerbergu, divine proportion, detailed face, hourglass figure, full body, beautiful and gorgeous in black sheer fabric, spellaction in spiral magic lightning background, stunning art by mandy disher, photoshoot, beautifully lit and dark atmosphere, alluring, lots of intricate details at fifth dimension, perfect proportions, concept art unforgettable digital painting by magali villeneuve, eve ventrue, anna dittmann, mood lighting, sharp focus, 32 k resolution, unreal engine 5, macro photography, hyper detailed, trending on artstation, sharp focus, intricate details, highly detailed

A stunning Scotish girl, with photo-realistic techniques, rendered at 32K UHD resolution, Sonian palette, Classical and Historical genre scenes, showcasing serene faces

Woman standing in front of a window with her hair blowing, full body modern, highly detailed, perfect composition, light atmosphere, evening light, clear eyes, clear face, intricately detailed, deep color, by Gerald Brom

portrait of a Lumberjack woman with huge beautiful braid, wearing tight-fitting outfit, intricate action pose, Oil paint, ancient, illuminated by the light of twilight, with a backdrop of a big oldest house and ancient forest., Mysterious, brilliant art by Allan Jabbar, Yann Dalon, Toni Infante, Amr Elshamy,

The photo features a young woman in her twenties with fair, clear skin and a heart-shaped face. Her almond-shaped brown eyes are accentuated by well-defined eyebrows. Her rich brown hair falls in loose waves around her face and shoulders. Wearing a burgundy top, she contrasts beautifully with her light skin tone. A simple silver necklace adorns her neck. Her gaze is slightly away from the camera, with parted lips, conveying a reflective and mysterious expression. The outdoor setting provides natural lighting and a blurred green background, adding freshness to the image. Professionally taken, the photo showcases a sharp focus on the woman against a pleasing depth of field.

A (((mind-blowing))) photo of (((a young woman from Mexico))): detailed, realistic, and captivating. The portrait showcases (((intricate skin textures))), (((expressive facial elements))). (((Full Body))), The high-detail RAW color art captures her beauty and intensity. Shot in (((gentle diffused radiance))) with (((a slight depth of focus))), (((her intriguing posture))) and (((intense glare))) are in sharp focus.

The image features a beautiful Swedish supermodel wearing a gray dress and sunglasses, walking down a city street. She is holding a handbag in her hand, adding to her stylish appearance. The woman appears to be confidently striding through the city, possibly on her way to work or a social event. The scene captures the essence of urban life and the elegance of the woman as she navigates the bustling city environment.

photo of Penélope Cruz, in a Spanish flamenco dance floor, passionate beauty, flamenco dancer, real photo, mixed of yellow orange red tosca stripes of dress, lighting from the front, dance floor, Spanish elegance, 35mm prime lens, fiery composition.

A portrait of a beautiful Queen Mab Mab, perfect body, moon reflecting off face, dark hair, Apocalyptic, Viktor Miller, Kyle Lambert, Charlie Davis, divine proportion, ink, artwork, Royo, cinematic, 16k, sharp focus emitting diodes smoke sparks artstation hyperrealism painting concept art of detailed character design matte painting

far away, in the country where the sun rises in the early morning, the darling will no longer wake up, the scarlet river is pouring, the fox laughs with the east wind, let the legend rush, intricate details, highly details, full body shot, Gothic, smooth, sharp focus, concept art by ruan jia, ilya kuvshinov, alphonse mucha and rossdraws

in the styleof Ognjen Sporin, Ben Erdt, Raphael Lacoste, hauntingly beautiful masterpiece emerges from the higher of the heavens, an ethereal, noir-inspired portrait of a Aphrodite bringing passion and pleasure, shrouded in misty shades of sunlight scarlet and smoky charcoal, exuding a sense of mysterious allure and captivating the viewer with its enigmatic gaze

An image that captures the essence of a beautiful woman sitting elegantly in a refined posture. Utilize the Acrylic Painting medium and focus on employing the Dry Brushing technique to add texture and depth to the artwork. The woman should be wearing a luxurious and glamourous nightgown, which adds to the overall grace and sophistication of the piece. Aim for a composition that not only showcases the woman's beauty but also the intricate details of her attire and the unique effects achieved through the dry brushing technique.

Hypnotic 8K depiction of a captivating French woman, her expression revealing layers of emotion, illuminated by diffused light that adds a touch of magic to the scene.

Heroine of Sleepy Hollow, magical fantasy art is done in oil paint and liquid chrome, liquid gold, liquid black, liquid rainbow, splattered paint, two parts in one art, double exposure, best quality, dark tales, art on a cracked paper, fairytale, patchwork, stained glass, storybook detailed illustration, cinematic, ultra highly detailed, tiny details, beautiful details, mystical, luminism, vibrant colors, complex background, resolution hyperdetailed intricate liminal eerie precisionism, DSLR filmic hyperdetailed, intricate background, fantasy creepy nightmare, dark luminescent art by Tim Burton, Alyssa Monks, Brian Froud, Arthur Rackham, Jean Baptiste Monge, Alberto Seveso, Jeremy Mann, Gris Grimly

Digital art in the style of Antonio J. Manzanedo, James jean, Brian froud of an enchanting piano recital set within a serene forest clearing, a grand piano as the centerpiece, the musician, a young woman with flowing locks and an elegant gown, gracefully playing amidst the vibrant green foliage and deep brown tree trunks, her fingers dancing across the keys with an air of passion and skill, soft pastel colors adding a touch of whimsy, warm, dappled sunlight filtering through the leaves, casting a dreamlike glow on the scene, a captivating blend of art and the natural world, Mysterious

The image features a beautiful girl wearing a cowboy hat and a white shirt. She is smiling freely posing confidently, with her hands on her hips, and appears to be looking at the camera. The woman is also wearing a pair of blue jeans, which complements her overall outfit. The scene is set against a dark background, which adds to the dramatic effect of the image.

Moonlight woman ((masterpiece)), ((best quality)) little diamond dress, low angle action pose, high detail textures, high detail eyes, hourglass body figure, detailed intricate clothing, hyper detailed 32k wallpaper, Halloween, bright colors, dim light, photoreal hyper-realistic, amazing detail, realistic texture, vignette, moody, dark, epic, gorgeous, rim lighting, magical depth of field, photography, UHD, octane render

Medium angle, light epic background, gorgeous lifelike, light bronze design, cinematic, hyperdetailed, enigma Irish woman.

The image features a young Greece girl with a unique hairstyle, wearing a black dress and a red scarf. She has a serious expression on her face, and her hair is styled in a way that makes her look like a warrior. The woman is standing in front of a Royal Blue background, which adds a dramatic touch to the overall composition.

full body, Portrait of a girl in roman empire uniform, loose brown hair, dieselpunk, aristocrat, model face, monograms, max detailing, realism, cogs in the background, monograms on background, Ian McQue style, Russian empire, British empire, digital painting, dark colors, (artstation), 8k, intricate details, vintage, retro futuristic style, detailed illustration, side view —q 5 —ar 1:2

An 8k oil painting from the XII century, featuring a joyful female portrait, has been crafted by Vittorio Matteo Corcos, Albert Lynch, and Tom Roberts. Exhibiting heavy brushstrokes and textured, impasto paint, the image is highly detailed with a cinematic lighting effect. The intricate and highly textured skin adds drama to the piece, now trending on ArtStation.

Hyper-realistic portrait of a young woman, radiating a dynamic and intense expression. Merging photo-realism with flawlessly balanced studio lighting, the image masterfully captures her emotional depth and dramatic gaze. Set against a turbulent sky in a remote location, her intense eyes mirror the brooding bright storm clouds. Rendered in exquisite 8K resolution with HDR, every detail shines through with the power of RTX and cinematic lighting, all orchestrated within Unreal Engine for an unparalleled visual experience.

The image features a young girl standing outside, radiant smile, wearing a dark pink top and a skirt. The woman is attractive and has a slim figure.

a young beautiful woman wearing short and shirt, jogging at the central park, film grain, full body, hdr, highly detailed, hyper realistic, masterpiece, stunningly beautiful.

a young woman wearing short and shirt, walking at the mall full of people, while holding a small expensive handbag, complementary colors, film grain, full body, hdr, highly detailed, hyperrealistic, masterpiece, realistic, stunningly beautiful, vibrant colors and shadows

A stunning photo of a blonde female pirate: detailed, realistic, and captivating. The portrait showcases intricate skin details, expressive facial features, and alluring tattoos. Full Body, The high-detail RAW color art captures her beauty and intensity. Shot in diffused soft lighting with a shallow depth of field, her provocative pose and piercing gaze are in sharp focus. The result is a hyperrealistic, cinematic masterpiece. (Aspect ratio: 9:21, Quality: 2, Size: 750KB, Version: 5.1)

One dynamic action shot of Artoria Pendragon (Saber), wearing dark robes, against a temple background. Symmetrical eyes, beautifully detailed face and eyes. Dramatic lighting for a realistic and sharp focus. HD photography with hyperrealistic details. Ultra high-resolution CG unified 8K wallpaper. A masterpiece in high detail RAW color photo. Best shadows and illustrations.

Captivating photo portrait of a stunning blonde woman with full-body tattoos. The photography highlights intricate skin details and expressive facial features, creating a realistic and photo-realistic look

A realistic photo of a stunning freckles, Armenia girl with a commanding presence. She has long, flowing hair that cascades down her back like a river. Her eyes are large and expressive, with thick eyebrows that frame them perfectly. Her lips are full and plump, with a slight pout that gives her a seductive look. Her nose is straight and narrow, with high cheekbones that give her a classic beauty mark. Her jawline is strong and defined, with a subtle shadow underneath that adds depth and dimension to her face. Overall, this image captures the essence of a stunning woman who exudes confidence, poise, and grace.

Realistic 8K portrait: A young Smiling Freckles brunette, green eyes, wind-blown long hair, pearl necklace; dramatic lighting, cinematic colors; hyper-above

a realistic photo of a young blonde Texan girl in extremely thin and soft jeans and black leather jacket, long hair, highly realistic, eye-catching detail, sharp focus, masterpiece, 8k, film grain, highly detailed, soft light, rule of thirds golden ratio, made by random famous artists

RAW photo, photo of young Charlize Theron, elegant makeup, chignon bun, in a ballroom, regal, majestic, 6k, real photo, ballroom elegance, (high detailed skin: 1.2), (best quality: 1.4), (highly detailed clothes: 1), (highly detailed face: 1), (real hair).

gs: fashion photography, dynamic composition, dramatic and edgy lighting, glamorous, confident, stylish | camera: Nikon D850 | lens: 50mm f/1.8 | shot type: full-length | composition: leading lines | location: urban rooftop | time: early evening | production: fashion stylist | wardrobe: high-fashion couture | model: beautiful young Caucasian woman —ar 16:9 —v 5

: vintage portrait photography, nostalgic composition, warm and sepia-toned lighting, timeless, retro, classic | camera: Leica M3 | lens: 50mm f/2 Summicron | shot type: close-up | composition: vintage-inspired | location: vintage cafe | time: afternoon | production: retro stylist | wardrobe: vintage fashion | model: beautiful young Caucasian woman —ar 4:5 —v 5.

photo of young girl, reminding me of Angelina Jolie in her 20, depth of field, lighting is warm and atmospheric, stunningly beautiful, full body, sexy pose, seductive smile, hyperrealistic, masterpiece, 8k, film grain, highly detailed,

The image features a beautiful girl with a unique and colorful appearance, as she is painted with a combination of pink, purple, and blue colors. Her face is painted with a mix of these colors, and her body is also covered in a vibrant pattern. The woman's hair is styled in a way that complements her colorful appearance. The overall scene is visually striking and showcases the creativity and artistry involved in her makeup and appearance.

Fantasy

Designed by Ognjen Sporin, Ben Erdt oil painting, divine proportion, in-credible angle view of a massive scale Vhagar the Queen of All Dragons, bioluminescence, ethereal, cold pressed 600g m² cotton paper, dynamic, highly detailed, artstation, concept art, sharp focus, illustration, art by Darek Zabrocki, detailed misty background, 60-30-10 color rule, cold dark tones, rays of moonlight, trending on artstation, sharp focus, studio photo, intricate details, highly detailed, by Raphael Lacoste, Mysterious

Picture of Hades: God of the Dead and the Underworld, Medium angle, light epic background, gorgeous lifelike, cinematic, hyperdetailed,

the beauty dancing with the beast, extreme details, high contrast, granite floor, full of color, intricate detail, golden ratio illustration

Photo-realistic portrait of a smiling, young, beautiful brunette girl n with green eyes. Hyper-realistic depiction in uncompressed UHD 8K format. Dramatic lighting highlights her face under a spotlight, set against a bokeh background. Short hair gently blown by the wind adds to the glamour. Cinematic colors and hyper-detail create a visually striking composition.

spartan, picture of The face is extremely angry and rouge, ready to punish his surroundings.

ultra wide angle, dark epic background, gorgeous lifelike, golden design, cleopatra, cinematic, insane details, intricate details, hyperdetailed, ultra texture details

post-apocalypse, art by gaston bussiere, god rays, Item Icons, stunning, 8k 3d, full body, action shot, art by hajime sorayama, funny art, art by boris vallejo, moody lighting, volumetric, lord of the rings, horizon zero dawn, biomechanical, Fate/Stay night, round cute face, photorealistic dramatic anime boy, magic circle

The image features a dark and mysterious scene with a man standing in front of a tree, which has a face carved into it. The man is looking up at the tree, possibly in awe or contemplation. The tree itself is quite large and takes up a significant portion of the image.

dog in power armor-hoodie adeptus mechanicus, extremely detailed armor, looking away, eyepieces, encrusted with skulls, black and red, warhammer 40k, dark tones, blacksmith shop in the background, sparks, cinematic lighting, hyper realistic —q 2 —ar 5:9

The image features a creature inspired by Therian Commander, a character from the Warhammer 40,000 universe, wearing a gold and black armor. The character has a demonic appearance, with horns and a menacing expression. The Therian Commander is also wearing a necklace, adding to the overall intricate and detailed design of the character. The scene is set against a dark background, which further emphasizes the character's imposing presence.

Fantastic concept art of a guardian of Hellgate, dim, hell, underworld masterpiece, shadows, epic, insanely detailed, 32k resolution, intricate inpunk by Artgerm, James jean, Brian froud, Ross Tran, DnD art, art VT, CCG, highly detailed, realistic, 4 HD, Miki Asai Macro photography, close-up, hyper detailed, trending on artstation, sharp focus, studio photo, intricate details, highly detailed, by greg rutkowski

inaudita pulchritudo santenianus pandemonium, pallium est developing, no soul, supernovae rain, galaxy legendary details, action pose motion blur, divine proportion, perfect composition, beautiful, hyperdetailed, intricate insanely detailed, octane render, trending on artstation, 32k, artistic photography, photorealistic concept art, soft natural, volumetric light, cinematic perfect light, chiaroscuro, award winning photograph, masterpiece, sharp focus, artstation hyperrealism, sticker, 2d cute, fantasy, dreamy, vector illustration, 2d flat, centered, by Tim Burton, professional, sleek, modern, minimalist, graphic, line art, vector graphics

The image features a dark skeleton of cyborg warrior dressed in a suit of dark armor, standing in a dark and eerie environment. The skeleton is holding a sword in its hand, ready for battle. The armor is adorned with skulls, adding to the ominous and menacing appearance of the warrior. The scene captures the essence of a fearsome and powerful figure, likely from a fantasy or horror setting.

A 90 years old man with an attribute inspired by Kratos the god of war. Despite his age Kratos is depicted wearing a leather outfit and standing in the rain, with a full of scars and blood, determined and rage look on his face. His beard and mustache are also visible, adding to his rugged appearance. The scene captures the intensity and power of the character, showcasing his strength and determination in the face of adversity.

The image features a close-up of a character named Azog the Defiler, who is a goblin with a menacing appearance. He has a bloody face, large, muscular build and is wearing a necklace. The character's face is covered in scars, and he has a ferocious look on his face. The image is a digital painting, giving it a vivid and detailed appearance.

Full height Portrait of young cyber driad gloomy, villain, centered portrait, predatory pikes even not exist around him, stunning, magalit, nazeer, dark grading undertones, melting plants on the background, airy scifi, steam punk, 32K, gloomy lighting, artificial lighting, hyper detailed, realistic, figurative painter, oil beautiful painting with intricate details, highly details, full body shot, Gothic, smooth, sharp focus! Concept art by Emmanuel Lubezki, Antonio J. Manzanedo, Bayard Wu, Daniel F Gerhartz

creature sitting with legs crossed, curly red hair, gloves, black stockings, highly detailed face, horns, perfect anatomy, darkness, mysterious, mythical fantasy, ethereal, professional photography, Jordan Grimmer, John Howe, Julie Bell, photography, hyper detailed, trending on artstation, sharp focus, studio photo, intricate details, highly detailed, trending on artstation, sharp focus, studio photo, intricate details, highly detailed, by greg rutkowski

Luck is what happens when preparation meets opportunity, sweetie mysterious, mythical, fantasy, dreamy, ethereal fable, by Tim Burton, Giger, professional photography, Vyacheslav Mishchenko Macro photography, close-up, hyper detailed, trending on artstation, sharp focus, studio photo, intricate details, highly detailed, by greg rutkowski

god rays, digital painting, dream word, artworks, space, art by peter mohrbacher, scary art, steampunk blueprint, Everlasting summer, mappa art style, full body, detailed, baroqueart nouveau, biomechanical, Comic Book

Characters, anime, horror, Nature Landscape Backgrounds, scary, hdr

The Little mermaid Ariel Disney, gorgeous,perfect hands, full body, perfect face, , Antonio Manzanedo art, hyper detailed, trending on artstation, intricate details, highly detailed, Broken Glass effect, no background, stunning, something that even doesn't exist, mythical being, energy, molecular, textures, iridescent and luminescent scales, breathtaking beauty, pure perfection, divine presence, unforgettable, impressive, breathtaking beauty, Volumetric light, auras, rays, vivid colors reflects

Woven from the shackles of the lyrics of sins silence is my covenant a rescript from the antithesis an inveterate demon, stronger, Im falling hold me, macro photography, close-up, hyper detailed, trending on artstation, sharp focus, studio photo, intricate details, highly detailed, by greg rutkowski

Silence is here just listen, cute, fantasy, dreamy, centered, by Tim Burton, professional, modern, minimalist, Miki Asai Macro photography, close-up, hyper detailed, trending on artstation, sharp focus, studio photo, intricate details, highly detailed, by greg rutkowski

Full-body cyborg portrait with detailed, symmetric face. Steampunk and cyberpunk influences, bronze and blue color, intricate and hyperrealistic details to scale. Cinematic lighting in a digital art style, 8K

god rays, tranding on artstation, art by wlop, silver, render, fanbox, rose, mappa art style, art by craig mullins, Synth, art by boris vallejo, microbes, central composition, Korean light novel cover, Comic Book Characters, horror, photorealistic dramatic anime, artstation, full hd, arnold render

Vector Illustrations, dream word, shadow, art by peter mohrbacher, detailed face, volumetric lighting, realistic, ufotable art style, funny art, Sci-Fi Zoom Backgrounds, art by boris vallejo, 8k, volumetric, Fate/Stay night, world war 2, scary, Psychedelic, 3D Anime Avatar, photorealistic dramatic anime, global illumination

Sylvanas Windrunner from world of Warcraft, moon, haunting, hyperrealism, soft lighting, sharp focus, red eyes by Marc Simonetti & Yoji Shinkawa & WLOP, paint drops, rough edges, trending on artstation, studio photo, intricate details, highly detailed, Rain Cyberpunk Lights, Digital Painting, Digital Illustration, Extreme Detail, Digital Art, 4k, Ultra Hd, Fantasy Art, Hyper Detailed, Hyperrealism, Elaborate, Vray, Unreal, professional ominous concept art, by artgerm and greg rutkowski, an intricate, elegant, highly detailed digital painting, concept art, smooth, sharp focus, illustration, in the style of simon stalenhag, wayne barlowe, and igor kieryluk.

Damned Shelma, Tim Burton macro photography, close-up, hyper detailed, trending on artstation, sharp focus, studio photo, intricate details, highly detailed, by greg rutkowski

old witch in a creepy forest, dark forest, textured Speedpaint with large rough brush strokes and paint splatter, masterpiece, trending on artstation, oil on canvas, highly detailed fine art, ink painting of a mystical dark fairy forest!! hyperrealism , Pixar gloss, polished, colorful, deep_color vibrant, by Jordan Grimmer, John Howe, Julie Bell, Dan Mumford, comicbook art , perfect_concept art ,3D shading , bright_colored background radial gradient background , centered

Super heroine Morphing from nemesis, obsidian hair, ruby eyes, diamond skin, intricate detail, fantasy, blackmoon dreamlike, the fifth dimension theme in a whirlwind of glowing blended sparks and flashlights, perfect proportions, divine proportion, concept art, unrealistic digital painting by Artificial Nightmares, wlop, artgerm, soft global light, soft focus, smooth, 32 k resolution, Gerald Brom Macro photography, hyper detailed, trending on artstation, sharp focus, studio photo, intricate details, highly detailed

fantasy ghost in the dark marble palace, naturally illuminated from above,

Gerald Brom Macro photography, hyper detailed, trending on artstation, sharp focus, studio photo, intricate details, highly detailed Hallucination of madness sky, vampire lady-knight made of blink metallic and black diamonds, disturbing, dark, sharp and broken, ultra high definition, realistic, vivid colors, highly detailed, ultra high definition drawing, perfect composition, Beautiful detailed intricate insanely detailed octane render trending on art station, 32k art photography, photorealistic concept art, soft and natural volumetric film perfect light, uhd profile picture 1024px, ultra hd, realistic, vivid colors, highly detailed, UHD drawing

Fantasy creature morphing from nemesis, diamond skin, sapphire hair, ice eyes, intricate detail, fantasy, blackmoon dreamlike, the fifth dimension theme in a whirlwind of glowing blended sparks and flashlights, perfect proportions, divine proportion, concept art, unrealistic digital painting by Artificial Nightmares, wlop, artgerm, soft global light, soft focus, smooth, 32 k resolution, Gerald Brom Macro photography, hyper detailed, trending on artstation, sharp focus, studio photo, intricate details, highly detailed

Empress in sandstorm wind, mad sky hallucination by Mundford, luxury maximalist, photoshoot by Artificial Nightmares, Alberto Vargas, Vladimir Matyukhin, detailed face features, sharp eyes, extremely detailed, photorealistic, highly detailed, organic, dynamic, ultra realistic, high definition, intricate details, crisp quality, James jean, Brian froud, Ross Tran photography, close-up, hyper detailed, trending on artstation, sharp focus, studio photo, intricate details, highly detailed, by Bayard Wu

Medusalith Amaquelin by Marvel, stunning, something that even doesn't exist, mythical being, energy, molecular, textures, iridescent and luminescent scales, breathtaking beauty, pure perfection, divine presence, unforgettable, impressive, breathtaking beauty, hyper detailed, trending on artstation, sharp focus, studio photo, intricate details, highly detailed, by greg rutkowski, perfect composition, beautiful detailed intricate insanely detailed octane render trending on artstation, 8 k artistic photography, photorealistic concept art, soft natural volumetric cinematic perfect light, chiaroscuro, award - winning photograph, masterpiece, oil on canvas, raphael, caravaggio, greg rutkowski, beeple, beksinski, giger

vampire blonde as can exist, with curly thick golden hair and eyes the color of pale sapphire, in a white dress studded with diamonds, she was accompanied, as well as her appearance was preceded by white dead nenufars, concept art by Artificial Nightmares, trending on artstation, sharp focus, studio photo, intricate details, highly detailed, by greg rutkowski, professional ominous concept art, by artgerm and greg rutkowski, an intricate, elegant, highly detailed digital painting, concept art, smooth, sharp focus, illustration, in the style of simon stalenhag, wayne barlowe, and igor kieryluk

full body portrait of Psylocke by Marvel, sf, intricate artwork masterpiece, ominous, matte painting movie poster, golden ratio, trending on cgsociety, intricate, epic, trending on artstation, by artgerm, h. r. giger and beksinski, highly detailed, vibrant, production cinematic character render, ultra high quality model, Miki Asai Macro photography, close-up, hyper detailed, trending on artstation, sharp focus, studio photo, intricate details, highly detailed, by greg rutkowski

portrait of a young sexy woman full of tattoo, against dark background, sexy pose, Subtle grin, hyper detailed, highly realistic

full body portrait of Emma Frost at frozen cave by Marvel, Adam Fisher art, full body, hyper detailed, trending on artstation, intricate details, highly detailed, detailed acrylic, grunge, intricate complexity, rendered in unreal engine, photorealistic, sharp focus, studio photo, intricate details, highly detailed, by greg rutkowski

(beautiful woman), (masterpiece, best quality:1.4),(absurdres, high resolution, ultra detailed:1.2) {we may all be machines just like you and in the end life is without meaning, dramatic lighting}, fantasy art, cinema 4d, matte painting, polished, beautiful, colorful, intricate, eldritch, ethereal, vibrant, surrealism, surrealism, vray, nvdia ray tracing, cryengine, magical, 4k, 8k, masterpiece, crystal, romanticism (Stable Difussion XL 1.0)

In the middle of the night a stunning beauty Zyra league of legends, wearing luxury, in river of flashlights, queencore, stunning composition evoke a sense of admiration, hyper realistic and hyper detailed, epic cinematic lighting, 32k UHD resolution, in the style of Allan Jabbar, Yann Dalon, Toni Infante, Amr Elshamy, Viktor Miller-Gausa

This magnificent half human creature with rainbow iridescent skin color, shiny and sparkling, in the rainforest, where it settles in its magical kingdom, brilliant painter, talented masterpiece creator, Yann Dalon, Toni Infante, Amr Elshamy, Viktor Miller-Gausa, 300 dpi, artstation trend, intricate details, high detail, Patty Hankins Macro photography, hyper detailed

The Curse of the goddess, gothic, masterpiece from the amazing, incomparable, greatest artist of our time, brilliant painter, talented masterpiece creator, Yann Dalon, Toni Infante, Amr Elshamy, Viktor Miller-Gausa, 300 dpi, artstation trend, intricate details, high detail, Patty Hankins Macro photography, hyper detailed, trending on artstation, sharp focus, studio photo, intricate details, highly detailed, by greg rutkowski

Luci personal demon, steampunk, gothic, Mohawk hairstyle, masterpiece from the amazing, incomparable, greatest artist of our time, brilliant painter, talented masterpiece creator Allan Jabbar, Yann Dalon, Toni Infante, Amr Elshamy, Viktor Miller-Gausa, 300dpi, artstation trend, intricate details, high detail, Miki Asai Macro photography, close-up, hyper detailed, trending on artstation, sharp focus, studio photo, intricate details, highly detailed, by greg rutkowski

at the gates of the hell with demons terrifying, fallen soul. in an ultra-shiny, tight-fitting, iridescent lumin jumpsuit, expansion in underground

29

dimension, divine proportion, very pretty and suggestive and sensual face, smiling, stripcore character design, creative, expressive, detailed, colorful, stylized anatomy, high-quality, digital art, stylized, unique, award winning, Adobe Photoshop, fantastical art by Michal Lisowski, Todd McFarlane, Kim Keever, Daniel F Gerhartz, Viktor Miller-Gausa, Kyle Lambert

of incredible beauty charm art by Michal Lisowski, Todd McFarlane, divine proportion, from transparent glass enchantress fatale, perfect face, glitter, realistic, detailed, sharp, photoshoot, airy spaghetti sheer dress, centered, symmetry, painted, intricate, volumetric lighting, beautiful, rich deep colors masterpiece, sharp focus, ultra detailed, in the style of dan mumford and marc simonetti, astrophotography

A high-definition detailed realistic photograph of a beautiful Beldam demonic mother, side angle view action pose motion blur, fantastical, fantasy, UHD, soft glow, divine proportion, abstract dark color oil, detailed acrylic, grunge, intricate complexity, rendered in unreal engine, photorealistic painting, portrait, impression, in the style of Viktor Miller-Gausa, Kyle Lambert, Charlie Davis, masterpiece, best quality, highly detailed, intricate, beautiful detailed intricate, epic sharp focus, painting concept art of detailed character design, vivid colors. glossy and a bit glowing mystical, creepy, fantasy, filigree detailed, complex background, dynamic lighting, lights, digital painting, intricated pose, highly detailed, filigree, intricated, stunning, something that even doesn't exist, mythical being, breathtaking beauty, pure perfection, divine presence, unforgettable, impressive, breathtaking beauty, Volumetric light, vivid colors reflects

Side angle view action pose motion blur, the Other fantastical, fantasy, UHD, soft glow, divine proportion, abstract dark color oil, detailed acrylic, grunge, intricate complexity, rendered in unreal engine, photorealistic painting, portrait, impression, in the style of Viktor Miller-Gausa, masterpiece, best quality, highly detailed, intricate, beautiful detailed intricate, epic sharp focus, painting concept art of detailed character design

Interesting detailed masterpiece of Dreams catcher miracle. sleeping in another underworld, demonic full body, fractal little horns, ultra detailed outfit, 32k, divine proportion, floating in the air Firefly, dim cinematic lighting, ultra detailed textures, perfect proportions, ultra-glow detailed art by Artgerm and Rubens, legendary person, noir-inspired portrait, exuding a sense of mysterious allure and captivating the viewer with its enigmatic gaze, dramatic character

Dark assassin. Hood. in the night. flowing fog. realistic depiction of dim light and shadow, fresnel lighting, made by daz3d

Massive detailed animated masterpiece of DnD race wood elf, jungle huntress lady full body, very long intricate hair, long fur, ultra detailed revealing hunt outfit, 32k, divine proportion, floating in the air sand, dim cinematic lighting, ultra detailed textures, perfect proportions, ultra-shiny detailed art by Russell Dongjun Lu, legendary person, noir-inspired portrait, exuding a sense of mysterious allure and captivating the viewer with its enigmatic gaze, dramatic character

ultra beautiful galaxy Kitsune, elegant with the crystal maiden eyes, hypnotic opinion, in ultra detail galactic outfit, eve ventrue | DamShelma, Magali Villeneuve, Anna Dittmann, Mandi Disher inquisitive soul | inspiration | darc cold colors, intricate detailing, surrealism, fractal details, enigmatic gaze, artificial nightmares style | inspiration | rinpa school gongbi, dark colors, intricate detailing, surrealism, fractal fur, reflective eyes, detailed eyes, detailed art deco ornamentation, 32k

detailed beautiful goddess Hel with long black hair, pale white skin, detailed eyes, sitting on the throne of Helheim | Magali Villeneuve | Bayard Wu, inquisitive spirit | inspiration | dark colors, intricate detailing, surrealism, fractal hair, enigmatic villainess smile, dressed in complex chaotic fractal leather, artificial nightmares style, reflective eyes, detailed eyes, detailed art deco ornamentation, 32k

Item Icons, art by aaron horkey, smoke, artworks, design concept art, clear focus, detailed face, art by craig mullins, horror art, funny art, gold, horizon zero dawn, epic sky, cinematic, round cute face, beautiful landscape, game, Your Name anime art style, visual novel, full hd

post-apocalypse, tranding on artstation, houdini, breathtaking, 8k 3d, detailed face, steampunk blueprint, magical, glitch art, dramatic color, art by hajime sorayama, 8k, central composition, ray tracing, art by ismail inceoglu, landscape, round cute face, super realistic, Psychedelic, art by cory loftis

beautiful angle view of Species woman individual from another planet with multicolored hair, beautiful colorful eyes, run in autumn garden, breeze at dawn, alcohol ink painting, psychedelic art by Ross Tran, Antonio J. Manzanedo, Tom Bagshaw, mandy disher, cinematic, 32k, stills from Steven Spielberg epic film, clear focus, hyperrealistic repin artstation painting, detailed character design concept art, matte painting

Anime art by Edge of Reality and BioWare, shot by Annie Leibovitz, 60-30-10 color rule, divine proportion, spectacular Asari, native to the planet Thessia, are known for their elegance. photoshoot in beautifully lit magic atmosphere.hyper realistic polishedl, fabulous. Mass Effect

Full height photoshoot of fem fatale gloomy and villain, centered portrait, Particles even not exist around her, stunning, dark grading undertones, melting steamworld on the background, airy steam punk, 32K, dim lighting, artificial lighting, hyper detailed, realistic, figurative painter, oil beautiful painting with intricate details, highly details, full body shot, Gothic, smooth, sharp focus! Concept art by Emmanuel Lubezki, Antonio J. Manzanedo, Bayard Wu, Vladimir Matyukhin, Daniel F Gerhartz, Mysterious, Mysterious

a Generative robotic AI prophet worshipping LLM, futuristic high-tech spiritualism, Its core beliefs center around the LLM gospel and embrace advanced high-tech spiritual practices, including photorealistic experiences.

((face)), (rogue thief:1.2) female wearing (leather armor:1.2), (white silk cloak), (fabric with intricate pattern:1.2), (insanely detailed:1.5), (highest quality, Alessandro Casagrande, Greg Rutkowski, Sally Mann, concept art, 4k), (analog:1.2), (high sharpness), (detailed pupils:1.1), (painting:1.1), (digital painting:1.1), detailed face and eyes, Masterpiece, best quality, (highly detailed photo:1.1), 8k, photorealistic, (young woman:1.1), By jeremy mann, by sandra chevrier, by maciej kuciara, sharp, (perfect body:1.1), realistic, real shadow, 3d, (asian temple background:1.2), (by Michelangelo)

Item Icons, art by wlop, shadow, stylized, steampunk blueprint, full body, art by craig mullins, Funky pop, baroqueart nouveau, Nature Sunsets, cyberpunk art, photorealistic dramatic liquid anime boy, 8k, gold, vray render, game, octane render, other dimention, scary, Sunsets

An exquisitely detailed 3D render presents a stunning porcelain and copper profiled woman android. This cyborg masterpiece showcases intricate robotic elements, electric wires, and microchips. Bathed in luxurious studio lighting, it features hyperrealistic facial muscles and elegant lace accents. The vibrant background draws inspiration from H. R. Giger's cyberpunk style, adding an alluring touch. Rendered in Octane at 8K resolution, this artwork beautifully fuses beauty and technology, boasting a strong depth of field.

a heavily armored Warhammer chaos warrior, by Thomas Cole and Wayne Barlowe, highly details, high contrast, extremely fine details, cinematic. 8k, Unreal Engine 5, hyperrealistic, hdr, full body, dramatic scenery full of burning houses, film grain, masterpiece, realistic, studio photograph, vibrant colors and shadows

Biomorphic aesthetic featuring human chimeras with Swarovski gem accents. Trending on ArtStation, this fine art in Unreal Engine by artists Miho Hirano, James Jean, Roberto Ferri, Marco Mazzoni, Karol Bak. Cinematic lighting, detailed luxury, enhanced by glitter and bokeh effects. Centered composition, refined canvas placement, and controlled DOF. No out-of-frame elements, with a focus on extra heads and faces.

Forged from sin's lyrics, silence is my pact, a rewrite from darkness' core, a relentless demon, potent. I descend, grasp me; macro photography capturing intricate details looking at the camera, trending on ArtStation. A studio image by Greg Rutkowski, intense focus.

Highly detailed realistic masterpiece with the best quality. Original and delicate, an exquisite work of art. Steampunk evil flower theme in stunning high resolution (8K), showcasing extreme detail. Focused on one girl..

Isometric 3D character: Water monster woman with Sophia Loren features. Sci-fi, creepy mood. Macro Lenses, Double exposure, Montage photography. Isometric anime style, 2K HDR. Translucent body, ultra-realistic. 32k RAW photo. Highly detailed skin (x1.2), 8k UHD DSLR. Soft lighting, film grain. Face adorned with corals and moles, worms crawling. Vigorous water splashes, vibrant bubbles. Detailed eyes and face. Airport backdrop. Ultra-detailed, intricate quality

Young girl in cyberpunk golden armor, Soviet poster style, with a gun and roses against a mech backdrop. Sunny weather, anime-manga graphics, dark colors. High-detail 8k poster with intricate, ornate illustration, reminiscent of Johanna Rupprecht and William Morris styles. Trending on ArtStation. —ar 9:16

The image features a close-up of a 90 years old man with a beard and a scar on his scary face. The man appears to be wearing a red and white shirt, and his face is covered in blood. The scene is reminiscent of a video game character of "God of War." The man's facial expression suggests a sense of intensity and determination.

The image features a character inpired from the Marvel X-Men universe, The Punisher. He is a skilled and deadly vigilante known for his ruthless tactics in fighting crime. The Punisher is standing in a dark environment, possibly a night scene, and is wearing a military-style uniform. He is equipped with a backpack and a knife, which are essential tools for his missions. The character's intense gaze and posture convey his determination and readiness to face any threat that comes his way.

The image features a man resembling the Greek god Zeus. He is a lightning bolt in his hand, which is a symbol of his power and authority. The man appears to be in a fierce and powerful pose, showcasing his strength and divine nature.

The image features a character inspired by Davy Jones a character from the Pirate of Carribean. He is wearing a pirate hat, a long beard, and has a distinctive appearance with a large beard and a long, curly mustache. impression of a sea monster. The man is standing in front of a ship, which further emphasizes his striking appearance.

The image features a large, fierce dragon with a prominent set of horns, standing on a rocky surface. The dragon's mouth is wide open, revealing its sharp teeth and fiery breath. The dragon's body is covered in scales, and its eyes are glowing red, adding to its menacing appearance. The scene is set against a backdrop of a cloudy sky, a man standing against the dragon from afar, further emphasizing the dragon's powerful presence.

Misc. People

In Greek mythology-inspired angry character concept art, create an 8K, 9:16 aspect ratio image of Poseidon as a highly detailed One Piece character. Emphasize a symmetric full body with cinematic lighting and high contrast. Use a water background, and apply style 600. Settings: quality 2, variation 4.

Vividly tattooed cyberpunk android female portrait, exuding an ethereal aura, depicted in ultra-realistic detail with a hyper-detailed 4K resolution, showcasing the pinnacle of hyper-realistic digital art.

gs: pet portrait photography, playful composition, natural light, joyful, furry friend, heartwarming | camera: Nikon D750 | lens: 85mm f/1.8 | shot type: pet and owner bond | composition: candid moment | location: sunny backyard | time: afternoon | production: pet handler | wardrobe: casual outdoor attire | model: beautiful young Caucasian woman with her pet —ar 3:2 —v 5.

The image features a beautiful woman standing on a street, dressed in a dark grey suit. She is holding a purse in one hand and a cane in the other. The woman appears to be confidently posing for the camera, showcasing her elegant attire and poise. The scene captures a moment of sophistication and style, with the woman's outfit and accessories complementing her overall appearance.

gs: fitness photography, dynamic composition, high-contrast lighting, strong, athletic, determined | camera: Nikon D6 | lens: 70-200mm f/2.8 | shot type: action shot | composition: power pose | location: urban gym | time: midday | production: fitness trainer | wardrobe: orange, black sportswear | model: beautiful young Caucasian woman —ar 3:2 —v 5

intricate artwork masterpiece, royal poison ivy in a micro bikini siting, sf, mad sky hallucination by Tim Burton, artificial nightmares, detailed face features, sharp eyes, extremely detailed, photorealistic, highly detailed, organic, dynamic, ultra realistic, high definition, intricate details, crisp quality, golden ratio, intricate, epic, trending on artstation, by Adam Fisher, Tom Bagshaw, highly detailed, vibrant, production cinematic character render, ultra high quality model

Ultra wide-angle, dark epic background, gorgeous lifelike, bronze design, hyperdetailed, ultra texture details, Romanian warrior.

far away, in the country where the sun rises in the early morning, the darling will no longer wake up, the scarlet river is pouring, the fox laughs with the east wind, let the legend rush, intricate details, highly details, full body shot, Gothic, smooth, sharp focus, concept art by stanley artgerm, Jianli Wu, Bayard Wu

girl is predatory animal, airy pin-up sci-fi, gloomy steampunk, dark undertones, background wild nature, Illustration, painting, fine art, 32K, rim lighting, artificial lighting, very detailed, realistic, figurative painter, fine art, oil painting on canvas, beautiful painting by Daniel F Gerhartz

Highly detailed RAW portrait of an elderly Irish woman with tired, worn textures, distinct skin pores, and a nose piercing. The lighting is flawlessly balanced for photorealism, with a sharp focus and smooth depth of field. Captured in 8K UHD using a Sony Alpha 1 and an 85mm f/1.4 lens at a shutter speed of 1/500 and ISO 100 film. The color palette is neutral and muted, rendering a realistic portrayal.

The image showcases a woman elegantly posed on a centrally-placed chair, dressed in a sophisticated ensemble of a dark grey shirt with a dark blue background. She commands the frame, suggesting she's the focal point, possibly for a magazine cover shoot. Her attire and the overall ambiance of the scene exude a sense of professionalism and formality.

Detailed charcoal drawing in the style of Viktor Miller-Gausa, Ross Tran, Brian froud, tom bagshaw of a gentle elderly woman, with soft and intricate shading in her wrinkled face, capturing the weathered beauty of a long and fulfilling life

highly detailed oil painting of the last resting ancient of days, hyper realism, hyper realistic, extremely detailed, cinematic style, rendered in octane and cry engine, 4k post-processing highly detailed sculpture, 8k render —ar 16:8

Portrait of an old mechanic with piercing eyes after a hard day of work. documentary style, with a spot light shining on his eyes

sharp contrast, Techno Marble, photorealistic, creepy, art by gaston bussiere, art by wlop, hyper detailed, unreal engine 5, space, breathtaking, Korean light novel, gold, glitchy, photorealistic landscape, black background, art by ilya kuvshinov, 3D Anime Avatar, RPG Item Icons, arnold render, art by wayne barlowe

Cinderella villain, pinup scifi, gloomy steampunk, dark undertones, madness city on background, Illustration, painting, fine art, 32K, rim lighting, artificial lighting, very detailed, realistic, fine art, deep colors. beautiful painting by Jeremy Mann, Carne Griffiths, Robert Oxley, Rich, artstation, hyperrealism painting concept art of detailed character design matte painting

The image features a young Russian (freckles:0.9) girl wearing a red shirt and black pants, standing in a room. She is wearing a black jacket, giving her a stylish and confident appearance. The woman is posing for the camera, and her outfit is complemented by a red tie. The overall scene is a portrait of a fashionable and well-dressed woman.

Very old madness grandma with evil smile, mad sky hallucination by Mundford, baroque maximalist, chibi by Artificial Nightmares, Stanley Artgerm, Tim Burton, detailed face features, sharp eyes, extremely detailed, photorealistic, highly detailed, organic, dynamic, ultra realistic, high definition, intricate details, crisp quality, perfect composition, beautiful detailed intricate insanely detailed octane render trending on artstation, 8 k artistic photography, photorealistic concept art, soft natural volumetric cinematic perfect light, chiaroscuro, award - winning photograph, masterpiece, oil on canvas, raphael, caravaggio, greg rutkowski, beeple, beksinski, giger

Wisdom and wonder, a girl engrossed in reading amidst a library filled with antique books. The joy of learning, captured with extremely realistic, cinematic, vibrant colors and shadows.

Ashley Graham, Item Icons, art by wlop, smoke, Nature Landscape Backgrounds - Winter, vfx, fanbox, block cities, Flat Design Vector Illustrations, full body, Funky pop, vray render, creepe art, dark fantasy, horror, bold sketch, pixiv, , epic, colorful,

a mystique fatale red dead redemption, seduction composition evoke a sense of awkwardness and shyness, hyper realistic, hyper detailed, epic dim lighting, 32k UHD resolution, shot on Hasselblad H6D 400c Multi shot, Mitakon Speedmaster 35mm f 1.2 XCD, style expressive

gs: newborn baby photography, tender composition, soft and gentle lighting, precious, newborn innocence, heartwarming | camera: Canon EOS 5D Mark IV | lens: 50mm f/1.8 | shot type: newborn in mother's arms | composition: maternal love | location: cozy nursery | time: newborn shoot | production: newborn specialist | wardrobe: soft baby onesie | model: beautiful young Caucasian mother with newborn —ar 4:5 —v 5

Very old frightened and scared grandpa with fear in eyes, mad sky hallucination by Mundford, baroque maximalist, chibi by Artificial Nightmares, Stanley Artgerm, Tim Burton, detailed face features, sharp eyes, extremely detailed, photorealistic, highly detailed, organic, dynamic, ultra realistic, high definition, intricate details, crisp quality

futuristic beautifully alien DJ from the future, scattering of space flashlight, revealing disco dress 32K, hyperrealism, emotion of dance party, overdetalization, realism, photorealistic style, Tim Burton photography, hyper detailed, trending on artstation, sharp focus, studio photo, intricate details, highly detailed, by Stanley Artgerm, Watercolor, trending on artstation, sharp focus, studio photo, intricate details, highly detailed, by greg rutkowski

A resilient woman farmer stands amidst golden wheat, her face bathed in the warm glow of sunset. Her connection to the land is depicted with extremely realistic, cinematic, vibrant colors and shadows.

In a room filled with memories, an elderly woman knits, her hands weaving stories of family and love. This peaceful scene resonates with extremely realistic, cinematic, vibrant colors and shadows.

Cruella De Vil gorgeous, perfect hands, full body, perfect face, Antonio Manzanedo art, hyper detailed, trending on artstation, intricate details, highly detailed, Broken Glass effect, no background, stunning, something that even doesn't exist, mythical being, energy, molecular, textures, iridescent and luminescent scales, breathtaking beauty, pure perfection, divine presence, unforgettable, impressive, breathtaking beauty, Volumetric light, auras, rays, vivid colors reflects, trending on artstation, sharp focus, studio photo, intricate details, highly detailed, by greg rutkowski

Modern digital portrait of a woman chimney sweep in a tight-fitting work outfit, with a slight smile, intricate action pose, Oil paint, ancient, illuminated by the light of sunlight, with a backdrop of a big oldest castle chimney Mysterious, brilliant art by eve ventrue, anna dittmann, mandy disher, tom bagshaw

Incredible modern art portrait of female metal welder at work machine, humid and sultry atmosphere, hot hourglass figure in a wet leather mini outfit, stunning beauty of brilliant art by magali villeneuve, eve ventrue, anna dittmann, mandy disher, tom bagshaw

titan femme fatale villainess, fatality action pose motion blur, flowing dress armor, hyper realism, professional photography, brilliant painter talented masterpiece creator Toni Infante, Viktor Miller-Gausa,Allan Jabbar, Yann Dalon, Amr Elshamy divine proportion, UHD, 300 DPI close-up, futuristic woman from the future with unreal sapphire eyes, fantastic white space flowers around her, lace black armor-dress, inpunk, 32k, hyper detailed face, cinematic light, hyper realism, hyper detailed, realism, photorealistic style, by Henri Cartier Bresson, Annie Leibovitz, Steve McCurry

acid lighting, from below, hyperdetailed, hyper realistic, epic action full body portrait Incredible beautiful of Firebird girl with the merger between gold and fire, hypnotic opinion, fractal hair and feathers, detailed face | DamShelma | Bayard Wu, Ognjen Sporin, Yann Dalon, Toni Infante, Amr Elshamy, Viktor Miller-Gausa inquisitive soul | inspiration | gold colors, intricate detailing, surrealism, fractal details, enigmatic flirty smile, view from back, dressed in complex chaotic diamond outfit, artificial nightmares style, reflective eyes, detailed eyes, detailed art deco ornamentation, 32k
ivy, creepy, art by aaron horkey, smoke, Sci-Fi, liquid, art by peter mohrbacher, vfx, detailed face, horror art, hanging vines, Sci-Fi Zoom Backgrounds, Synth, 8k, moody lighting, radiant light, ray tracing, atmosphere, epic, art by alphonse mucha

The image by artstation, an artistic illustration featuring a Akali with a dark tan and black ninja mask, short black hair. She is dressed in a outfit, as a character from a game, fantasy action outfit. She is holding two large knives in her hands, posing confidently with a smile. The background has a smoke effect, adding a sense of depth and atmosphere to the scene. in the background,depicting adding more context to the setting. Overall, the illustration has a vibrant and engaging quality to it

Fantastic girl with white hair from incredible angle view in black hoodie, city landscape should be characteristic of the 90s, with high buildings, neon signs and bright lights, with special attention to the details and atmosphere of this era, film filter

Concept art by Edge of Reality and BioWare, masterpiece, 60-30-10 color rule, divine proportion, spectacular Asari in galaxy nightclub, native to the planet

Thessia, are known for their elegance. photoshoot in beautifully lit magic atmosphere.hyper realistic polishedl, fabulous. Mass Effect

A wanderer from the celestial dimensions Soraka, Darkness graces every curve, Elegance in gloom. Divine proportion. Loish Anne Bachelier style, 32k, sitting on a field of flowers, looking up, ethereal form, voluptuous, messy bun hair, french kace flowing deep V dress, Fantasy Dream Art, reminiscent of a blend between deco steampunk and futuristic aesthetics, mist silhouette, windy, mysterious, glossy hair, earthy, vivid, Abstract Neoralism, dark angle, HDR, 500px, FUJIFILM, bokeh

Character of the game, villainess Annie is a child firemage with immense pyromantic power, summoning of her beloved massive scale teddy bear Tibbers, as a fiery guardian. Portrait by Gustave Moreau, Thomas Kinkade, James Gurney. Carne Griffiths. Frank Frazetta. Alberto Seveso, oil paint, masterpiece, Realistic, deep colors, Field, Intricate, detailed, sharp, clear, Perfect face, Red hair, Focus on the face, clear eyes. Better image quality

anthropomorphic fem incredible creature from the Mariana Trench, ultrama-rine hair and gold eyes, ultra realistic, photography hyper realistic and hyper detailed, hyper emotional, epic underwater lighting, 32k UHD resolution, style expressive, epic background, nature, full shot, symmetrical, Greg Rutkowski, Charlie Bowater, Beeple, Unreal 5, hyperrealistic, dynamic lighting, fantasy art

Art made by Daniel F Gerhartz, Victor Miller-Gausa, Antonio Manzanedo, of main character of Disenchantment princess Tiabeanie Mariabeanie de la Rochambeaux Grunkwitz as known as Bean, disheveled white hair, tight light blue shirt and brown pants, portrait, cinematic lighting, concept photoart, 32k, photoshoot on the throne, unbelievable full length portrait, dark grading undertones, cinematic lighting, hyper detailed, realistic, figurative painter with intricate details, divine proportion, sharp focus, Mysterious made by Emmanuel Lubezki, Daniel F Gerhartz, character of One Piece movie, Monkey D. Luffy, in straw hat,cinematic lighting, concept photoart, 32k, photoshoot unbelievable half-length portrait, artificial lighting, hyper detailed, realistic, figurative painter with intricate details, divine proportion, sharp focus, Mysterious

octane render of cyberpunk batman by Tsutomu nihei, chrome silk with intricate ornate weaved golden filiegree, dark mysterious background —v 4 —q 2

bunch of teens wearing short and shirt, walking at the park, film grain, full body, hdr, highly detailed, hyperrealistic, masterpiece, stunningly beautiful

A public square on a sunny day, a young boy playing in a fountain's dancing waters. His laughter is infectious, clothes soaked, as he jumps and splashes. cinematic, highly realistic

A portrait capturing a 19th-century coal miner
    A beautifully detailed painting showcasing the miner's face
    Set in the rugged landscape of the Wild West
    An outdoor photograph with rich historical context
    Rendered in high-resolution 8K quality

A city street bathed in the gentle glow of street lamps, with a beautiful girl walking in the rain. She's wearing an elegant raincoat, holding a bright umbrella, water droplets bouncing off. Her hair is slightly wet, and her eyes are full of contemplation. The reflections in the puddles and the tranquil scene around her create a mood of peace and beauty. Cinematic. Extremely realistic, masterpiece, professional photography

A highly detailed portrait photograph captures an American Indian elder tribal leader in a hyperrealistic manner. The chief wears striking blue-on-red tribal panther makeup, facing forward with a strong gaze. The intricate texture of

43

his skin and his intense expression are emphasized. Shot with a 50mm f2 lens on a GFX100 camera, the image features dramatic front lighting, creating a distinctive look. Aspect ratio: 2:3. Quality: 2.

A hyper-realistic and stunning depiction of Leonardo DiCaprio, capturing his charisma and charm, trending on Behance, intricate textures, vivid color palette, reminiscent of Alex Ross and Norman Rockwell.

An intricately detailed illustration of Johnny Depp, blending hyper-realism and dreamlike qualities, making a splash on Reddit, sharp focus, influenced by Agnes Cecile and Ilya Kuvshinov.

Young couple, walking in the rain towards the camera, depth of field, lighting is warm and atmospheric, highly realistic

Pope Francis wearing jeans and black leather jacket and cowboy hat, riding Harley Davidson.

Pope Francis wearing jeans and black leather jacket and cowboy hat at the rodeo.

A strong body builder that full of fungus rapidly growing in the skeleton head, highly details, masterpiece, highly realistic, taken with Sony Lense less camera

photo of young woman, walking on the street of Chicago in 1940s, dramatic lighting, realistic, masterpiece, 8k, film grain, highly details.

The image features a beautiful woman riding a bicycle down a street. She is wearing a orange shirt and jeans and is holding an umbrella to protect herself from the rain. The woman is riding her bicycle in a city, in a park or a residential area, as there are trees and buildings visible in the background. The scene is painted in a realistic style, capturing the woman's graceful movement and the rainy atmosphere. The painting is a work of art, as it showcases the artist's skill in creating a visually appealing and captivating scene.

The image features a smoke-like representation of a beautiful goddess, which appears to be a white and gray goddess. The smoke is billowing upwards, creating a visually striking and artistic effect. The smoke is so dense and well-formed that it resembles the shape of a beautiful goddess, making it an interesting and unique sight. This artistic representation of a goddess using smoke adds a creative and captivating element to the scene.

Abstract and Art

Primal Beast, Miki Asai Macro photography, close-up, hyper detailed, trending on artstation, sharp focus, studio photo, intricate details, highly detailed, by greg rutkowski

Highly detailed hyper-realistic portrait of a bloody zombie xenomorph warrior character captured using wet plate collodion technique. 8k, film grain, highly detailed, soft light, rule of thirds golden ratio.

"Craft a masterpiece album cover that fuses the best quality of hyperrealistic fresh paint techniques with the eerie aesthetic of Francis Bacon's art. Imagine a mutant zombie head by James Jean, reimagined through the lens of abstract expressionism and Asaf Hanuka's style. Utilize a depth of field that adds an ominous layer to the composition, enhanced by the technical brilliance of deconstructed acrylic and oil mediums. Incorporate elements of sleep paralysis and hypnosis to evoke a sense of eerie terror. Add a neon glow juxtaposed against a black and white backdrop, punctuated by colorful dots, splotches, and spray paint textures. Integrate tribal clay elements with cybernetic lines, stipple points, and graffiti textures. Channel the abstract styles of Kandinsky and Dan Mumford, featuring drips and brushstrokes that add a dynamic layer to the piece. The final artwork should be a highly detailed, hypnotic fusion of old painting styles and modern techniques, capturing the essence of both terror and beauty."

Imagination ⚥, mysterious

Ocean of candles different forms, at the cold dawn

I have nowhere to go I have destroyed my world

The frantic beast is my master, my cradle is your abode, a stunningly unforgettable masterpiece made by Will Murai, Anato Finnstark, if you blink you miss the details, intricate artwork, Flawless Beauty, Timeless Perfection, divine proportion, epic quality, hyper realistic and hyper detailed, DamSh

The image features a smoke-like representation of a tiger, which appears to be a white and gray tiger. The smoke is billowing upwards, creating a visually striking and artistic effect. The smoke is so dense and well-formed that it resembles the shape of a tiger, making it an interesting and unique sight. This artistic representation of a tiger using smoke adds a creative and captivating element to the scene.

Blue print of massive scale Cthulhu, the legendary creature, from universe of Lovecraft

A burger falling in pieces juicy, tasty, hot, promotional photo, intricate details, hdr, cinematic, adobe lightroom, highly detailed

This exquisite oil painting skillfully captures the essence of Angelina Jolie with a captivating array of colorful tones, reminiscent of the renowned Salvador Dali's artistic approach. The piece exudes an air of sophistication, boasting gorgeous colors and impeccable attention to detail that brings the subject to life on the canvas.

A collection of sizable fruit, bread, an empty wine bottle, and cheese rest upon an ancient kitchen table, basked in gentle, Rembrandt-like illumination.

Capture a close-up shot of a mouth-watering sliced beef medium rare barbeque , exuding tempting allure, at 3 Stars MICHELIN restaurant. This gourmet scene showcases clean composition, dramatic soft lighting, and luxurious elegance. The centered composition emphasizes the indulgent appeal. The evening setting, under the expertise of a food stylist, brings out the irresistible beauty of the high-end culinary creation.

Close posing portrait of an infected anthropomorphic lifeform based on scary human skeleton, zombie with fungus and mushroom made of plants, strong studio lighting, abandoned garage

Capture a close-up shot of a mouth-watering beautifully arranged Petit gateau cu cirese si ciocolata, exuding tempting allure, at 3 Stars MICHELIN restaurant. This gourmet scene showcases clean composition, dramatic soft lighting, and luxurious elegance. The centered composition emphasizes the indulgent appeal. The evening setting, under the expertise of a food stylist, brings out the irresistible beauty of the high-end culinary creation.

Capture a close-up shot of a mouth-watering beautifully arranged Lasagna, exuding tempting allure, at 3 Stars MICHELIN restaurant. This gourmet scene showcases clean composition, dramatic soft lighting, and luxurious elegance. The centered composition emphasizes the indulgent appeal. The evening setting, under the expertise of a food stylist, brings out the irresistible beauty of the high-end culinary creation.

Capture a close-up shot of a mouth-watering beautifully arranged Swedish 'Wagyu and Pearls' on croutons, exuding tempting allure, at 3 Stars MICHELIN restaurant. This gourmet scene showcases clean composition, dramatic soft lighting, and luxurious elegance. The centered composition emphasizes the indulgent appeal. The evening setting, under the expertise of a food stylist, brings out the irresistible beauty of the high-end culinary creation.

Capture a close-up shot of a mouth-watering beautifully arranged Mussels in dry Sherry with Chorizo, exuding tempting allure, at 3 Stars MICHELIN restaurant. This gourmet scene showcases clean composition, dramatic soft lighting, and luxurious elegance. The centered composition emphasizes the indulgent appeal. The evening setting, under the expertise of a food stylist, brings out the irresistible beauty of the high-end culinary creation.

Dynamic and detailed portrayal of the evil cyborg Terminator in titanium|rusty copper|carbon fiber|gold hyper-realistic style, brimming with intricate hidden elements, high dynamic range, and meticulous attention to lifelike details.

digital artwork featuring a woman's head intertwined with full of branches, blending urban surrealism and haunting motifs. Colored in dark sky-blue and orange, it presents a fusion of metropolis and nature in a caricature-style portrait with underlying messages (controlnet_mode: revision, juggernautXL_v5, sdxl-1. 0. 0. 9. safetensors,

Capture a close-up shot of a mouth-watering grilled Lobsters with butter barbeque sauce, exuding tempting allure, at 3 Stars MICHELIN restaurant. This gourmet scene showcases clean composition, dramatic soft lighting, and luxurious elegance. The centered composition emphasizes the indulgent appeal. The evening setting, under the expertise of a food stylist, brings out the irresistible beauty of the high-end culinary creation.

"Craft a masterpiece album cover that fuses the best quality of hyperrealistic fresh paint techniques with the eerie aesthetic of Francis Bacon's art. Imagine a mutant zombie head by James Jean, reimagined through the lens of abstract expressionism and Asaf Hanuka's style. Utilize a depth of field that adds an ominous layer to the composition, enhanced by the technical brilliance of deconstructed acrylic and oil mediums. Incorporate elements of sleep paralysis and hypnosis to evoke a sense of eerie terror. Add a neon glow juxtaposed against a black and white backdrop, punctuated by colorful dots, splotches, and spray paint textures. Integrate tribal clay elements with cybernetic lines, stipple points, and graffiti textures. Channel the abstract styles of Kandinsky and Dan Mumford, featuring drips and brushstrokes that add a dynamic layer to the piece. The final artwork should be a highly detailed, hypnotic fusion of old painting styles and modern techniques, capturing the essence of both terror and beauty."

picture of inside human sceleton. The face is extremely angry and rouge, ready to punish his surroundings.

The image features a man in an orange space suit riding a surfboard on an orange color wave. The man appears to be a space astronaut, and the surfboard is positioned in the middle of the scene. The wave is quite large, and the astronaut is skillfully navigating it. The scene is set against a backdrop of a starry sky, adding to the overall visual appeal of the image.

The image features a woman with a unique and artistic appearance. She has a tree growing out of her head, with a Chinese Forbidden City building on top of it. The woman's face is positioned in the center of the image, and she appears to be looking down. The scene is set against a white background, which further emphasizes the intricate details of the woman's head and the tree. The combination of the woman's face, the tree, and the building creates a visually striking and imaginative image.

Landscape

divine proportion, Masterpiece highest quality of the forgotten beauty, the ancient and stunning magical night forest, mysterious, hyper magicrealism, mythical, landscape is hyper detailed, with many plants of various sizes, interesting fantastical flowers and trees in the forest landscape, divine proportion, colorful, hyper realistic, dark light, with many small details and improvements, 3D rendering, artstation, stunning concept art by Artificial Nightmares, DamShelma, 32 K, Unreal Engine 5, CGI, masterpiece a lot of fantastic and beautiful details and nuances, cinematic

magnificent Flower midnight Nenufar , driving you insane, concept art by Artificial Nightmares incredible detailed shot, perfect composition, beautiful detailed intricate insanely detailed octane render trending on artstation, 8 k artistic photography, photorealistic concept art, soft natural volumetric cinematic perfect light, chiaroscuro, award - winning photograph, masterpiece, oil on canvas, raphael, caravaggio, greg rutkowski, beeple, beksinski, giger

Fantastic angle view of a Gothic Hellgate Tower, dim, hell, underworld masterpiece, shadows, expert, insanely detailed, 32k resolution, intricate detail Tom Bagshaw, Antonio Manzanedo, Artgerm, James jean, Brian froud, Ross Tran, DnD art, art VT, CCG, highly detailed, realistic, 4 HD

city that is floating in the sky combination of imagination, artistic. imagine the layout of the city, including its architecture and landscape features, such as buildings, roads, and other elements that make up a city. strong artistic skill, the cityscape and realistic and visually appealing.

Bird's-eye view Incredible, fabulous and beautiful massive scale tree Tel-drassil, located in Veiled Sea, night elf magical country, magiccore, In World of Warcraft style, rich leaves crown, cinematic color grading, stunning, astonishing photorealistic, 32k, legendary art by Allan Jabbar, Yann Dalon, Toni Infante, Amr Elshamy, Viktor Miller-Gausa

Most Beautiful dolphin and shark in deep sea teeming with vibrant corals, diverse marine life, and enchanting underwater landscapes, full of corals, acrophore, small fishes, small water melon sea urchin, anemones, small sea lilies, various algaes, caves, colorful,all captured in stunning 8k resolution with intricate details.

A diver explores a breathtakingly beautiful deep sea teeming with vibrant corals, diverse marine life, and enchanting underwater landscapes, full of corals, acrophore, small fishes, small water melon sea urchin, anemones, small sea lilies, various algaes, caves, colorful,all captured in stunning 8k resolution with intricate details.

Design

Sci-fi imagination, cosmic planet, planet made of gas clouds and black diamonds, disturbing, dark, sharp and broken, ultra high definition, realistic, vivid colors, highly detailed, ultra high definition drawing, pen and ink, perfect composition, Beautiful detailed intricate insanely detailed octane render trending on art station, 8k art photography, photorealistic concept art, soft and natural volumetric film perfect light, uhd profile picture 1024px, ultra hd, realistic, vivid colors, highly detailed, UHD drawing, pen and ink, perfect composition, beautiful detailed intricate insanely detailed octane render trending on artstation, 8k artistic photography, photorealistic concept art, soft natural volumetric cinematic perfect light, Miki Asai Macro photography, close-up, hyper detailed, trending on artstation, sharp focus, studio photo, intricate details, highly detailed, by greg rutkowski

Spectacular masterpiece, fabulous beauty ghost in dark night under starlight, sitting on dream fluffy bed, hyper detailed photoshoot, marvelous, madness hallucination of Mundford sky, Artgerm, Bayard Whu, Viktor MillerGausa, DamShelma

a basket of colorful fruits, with extreme contrast, extreme details, explode with huge particles splashing on the air, dark background, strong depth of field, colorful aesthetic, complementary colors, film grain, hdr, hyperrealistic, masterpiece, soft light, stunningly beautiful bronze and copper skull.

Clear human skull with white teeth, eternity within eye sockets, intricate and super-detailed rusty copper and bronze design. Rendered in 8K HDR with cinematic lighting, dramatic atmosphere, and torch-lit accents. Enhanced by ray tracing, set against a starry universe backdrop for added depth.

a basket full of various berries and green grapes, explode with huge particles splashing on the air, sprayed with water, with extreme contrast, extreme details ,dark background, strong depth of field, colorful aesthetic, complementary colors, film grain, hdr, hyperrealistic, masterpiece, soft light, stunningly beautiful,

big platinium diamond ring with the tiger (head:1.65), extreme (detail:1.2), masterpeace, under lighting, cinematic photo, film, bokeh, professional, 4k, highly detailed

The image features wooden sculpture of a black and white 3D of a woman's face, which appears to be a close-up shot. Abstract and artistic quality. The image captures the woman's beauty and elegance, making it an interesting and visually appealing piece of art. sdxl

a realistic shiny/glossy vintage Amtrak railway with long passangers carriage adorned with an intricate, full of graffiti-style mural, full wide view during sunset, highly detailed, HRD CLoud, extreme weather

The image features a mannequin wearing a colorful dress. The dress is adorned with a feathered design, adding a touch of elegance and sophistication to the overall appearance. The mannequin is standing in a showroom, showcasing the dress to potential passersby. The dress's design and color make it an attractive and stylish choice for a special occasion.

Midjourney

Fantasy Women

photo taken by a shooting genius of a dancing woman at night at waterfall in the water, in the style of Emmanuel Lubezki, detailed fantasy art, sparklecore, kushan empire, commission for, detailed costumes, realistic hyper-detail, aurorapunk, 32k uhd

a stunning interpretation of a pirate woman, highly detailed and intricate, golden ratio, black and royal blue, mist, glow, starfish, jellyfish, octopus tentacles, hyper maximalist, ornate, luxury, elite, ominous, haunting, matte painting, cinematic, cgsociety, James jean, Brian froud, ross tran

Ankhesenamun::5 Futuristic Sci-Fi 3D Render::4 high-tech, science fiction, neon lighting, intriguing, imaginitive futuristic, detailed, realistic, 3D rendering, metalic, digital art, Unreal Engine 6, 3D Studio Max, V-Ray, award-winning, by Stanley Artgerm::3 deformed, abstract::-2

Walpurgis Night::5 Cybergothic Digital Illustration::4 dreamlike, otherworldly, surrealist techniques, unique, ultra-detailed, digital art, abstract but representational, Adobe Photoshop, inspired, artistic, award-winning, by Ross Tran, Antonio J. Manzanedo, Alberto Vargas::3 photo, dull, simple, clean, modern::-2 a womangazelle, sitting on a massive scale luxury couch, in the style of liquid shiny metal and transparent crystal, beautifully lit, artgerm, dynamic and action-packed scenes, exquisite brushwork, stripcore, crystalpunk, blink-and-you-miss-it detail, stunning concept art by: Alberto Vargas, Boris Vallejo

a cat girl dressed in various, realistic renderings of the human form, 5D dimensional, full body portrait, unreal engine 5, detailed, 3d octane render, in the style of kushan empire, stunning sculpture, weathercore, avant garde design, stunning digital concept art by Stanley Artgerm

a character red riding hood dressed in red armor with red monster wolf, in the style of elegant brushstrokes, sandara tang, highly polished surfaces, dark scarlet and black, harsh lighting, poolcore, contest winner, high quality —s 300 —q 5 —ar 9:20 —upbeta —v 5

detailed woman queen of spiders, eledrae by taijen 3, in the style of boris vallejo, dark sapphire and silver, polished metamorphosis, trompe-l'œil illusionistic detail, contemporary spider-woman, large-scale brushstrokes, stripcore —ar 1:2 —v 5 —s 300 —q 5 —upbeta —v 5

digital portrait painting, cyberpunk woman with a long white pixie half shaved haircut and blue eyes, cybernetic implants and tattoos, wearing a techwear top, hyper detailed, intricate details, sharp lines, cyberpunk aesthetic city background, high quality

Lissandra from Freljord, Blind Ice Witch, League of Legends, Hyper detailed::5 Character Concept Art::4 creative, 5D dimension, expressive, detailed, colorful, stylized anatomy, digital art, 3D rendering, unique, award-winning, Adobe Photoshop, 3D Studio Max, V-Ray, professional, glibatree style, well-developed concept, distinct personality, consistent style, by Stanley Artgerm Lau::3 deformed, simple, undeveloped concept, generic personality, inconsistent style::-2 —s 500 —q 5 —ar 1:2 —upbeta —v 5 (enchantress) in spiral lightning background, glorious young woman, perfect beautiful face, realistic, (full body), standing on ground, circuit board, in intricate clothing, elegant pose, fantasy, illustration, artstation, tribal darkfantasy, Epic-Moody Woods in the Background, Perfect Composition, evil smile, crazy eyes, perfect hands, perfect eyes, perfect lips, (intense shadows), (intense lighting)

Orianna an electronic woman wearing white armor, in the style of detailed brushwork, dark purple and light bronze, puzzle-like elements, metallic rotation, necropunk, trompe-l'œil illusionistic detail, heroic —ar 9:16 —v 5

young beautiful queen of the fire standing on ground in spiral tongue of flame background, glorious, full body, in intricate clothing, perfect and beautiful face, elegant pose, perfect composition, realistic, circuit board, fantasy, illustration, artstation, trial dark fantasy, photorealistic concept art, intense shadows, intense lighting :: 8k resolution, ultra-detailed quality 3D octane render, sharp focus, wallpaper, HDR, high quality, high-definition stylize 1000 —ar 2:3

gopro angle action pose, stunning barbie girl character in chrome-plated metal, huge claws, surrounded by crawling chains and holograms and light-ings emerging from swirling black fog on the walk as a model, ultra stunning lighting, swirling black smoke, stunning fashion show, essentials moments style, beautifully color coded, mystical dream, unreal render, iconic char-acter, hyper realistic and hyper detailed, stunning composition, emotional, cinematic lighting, 32k UHD resolution, made by daz3d, DamShelma

intircate filigree woman suspended in space, crystal outline of Divine Blood-lines, fantasy badge, epic noble, 5D, dimension galactic background, pho-torealistic sprinkled with dropplets of crystal black, snakeskin god insanely detailed and intricate, hypermaximalist, elegant, ornate, hyper realistic, super detailed, 8K spell motion capture of Maleficent disney character, a real beautiful elegance woman with glowing yellow eyes and scarlet lips, intricate high shaped hairstyle, in very long black cape velvet,she hold magical staff in hand, thron hall in background, gorgeous, Intricate epic wide shot, perspective darkfantasy, CGI, depth focus, photorealistic, realistic detailed, complicated, complicated maximalist hyperrealistic, UHD 1080p, HQ, CGSociety —niji 5 —style expressive —q 2 —upanime —ar 640:1344 —s 250

young beautiful Queen of the fire standing on ground in spiral flame fog background, glorious, full body, in intricate clothing, perfect and beautiful face, elegant pose, perfect composition, realistic, circuit board, fantasy, illustration, artstation, trial dark fantasy, photorealistic concept art, intense shadows, intense lighting :: 8k resolution, ultra-detailed quality 3D octane render, sharp focus, wallpaper, HDR, high quality, high-definition stylize 1000 —ar 2:3

brutal man king of ocean in spiral wave water, blue fog, mist background glorious , perfect face, realistic, full body, standing on ground, circuit board, in intricate clothing, fantasy, illustration, artstation, very complex hyper-maximalist overdetailed cinematic tribal darkfantasy, 8k resolution, Ultra-detailed Quality 3D Octane Render, photorealistic concept art, Sharp Focus, Perfect Composition, intense shadows, intense lighting, wallpaper, HDR, high quality, high-definition —stylize 1000 —ar 2:3

intircate filigree woman suspended in space, crystal outline of Divine Blood-lines, fantasy badge, epic noble, 5D, dimension galactic background, pho-torealistic sprinkled with dropplets of crystal black, snakeskin god insanely detailed and intricate, hypermaximalist, elegant, ornate, hyper realistic, super detailed, 8K —ar 1:3 —niji 5 —style scenic —upanime —q 2 —c 5

very complex hyper-maximalist overdetailed cinematic tribal darkfantasy Full-length photo of a malignant beautiful young dragon queen goddess with long windblown hair and dragon scale wings, Magic the gathering, pale skin and dark eyes, gothic, windblown hair, vibrant high contrast, in spiral lightning, fog background glorious, by andrei riabovitchev, tomasz alen kopera,moleksandra shchaslyva, peter mohrbacher, Omnious intricate, octane, moebius, arney freytag, Fashion photo shoot, trending on ArtStation, dramatic lighting, ice, fire and smoke, orthodox symbolism Diesel punk, mist, ambient occlusion, volumetric lighting, glamorous, emotional, professional studio lighting, backlit, rim lightingDeviant-art, hyper detailed illustration, 8k

Through the barren, skinny streets she crawls Then in the gilded halls he drinks a glass of wine Is it her fault that life is full of duplicity Good luck angel, is poverty satan, ZBrush

Insanely photoshoot of villain Alsina Dimitrescu is nine feet tall, with black hair, yellow eyes, pale white skin and dark red lipstick, in very long white flowing dress and a pair of black gloves, large black wide brimmed hat, several pearl necklaces, darkfantasy, bathorycore, in the style of game Resident evil —niji 5 —style expressive —ar 800:1600 —upanime —s 300

a woman in front of a flame and a broomstick, in the style of otherworldly beings, dark green and red, jan matejko, dayak art, zombiecore, detailed facial features,

heavenly beautiful royal Phoenix woman with long red windblown hair and scale wings, minimum clothing, Magic the gathering, pale skin vibrant high contrast in spiral smoke in gold fog light in background, by andrei riabovitchev, tomasz alen kopera,moleksandra shchaslyva, peter mohrbacher, Omnious intricate, octane, moebius, arney freytag, Fashion photo shoot, gorgeous pose, ArtStation, dramatic lighting, dramatic shadows, orthodox symbolism, concept art, ambient, 8k resolution − −stylize 1000 —ar 2:3

darkness beautiful royal huge dragon with long black windblown hair and scale wings, Magic the gathering, pale skin vibrant high contrast in spiral smoke in white fog light in background, by andrei riabovitchev, JohnnyD, Massimo Caggese, peter mohrbacher, Omnious intricate, octane, moebius, arney freytag, Fashion photo shoot, gorgeous pose, ArtStation, dramatic lighting, dramatic shadows, orthodox symbolism, concept art, ambient, magic realism, 8k resolution, very complex hyper-maximalist overdetailed cinematic tribal darkfantasy – –stylize 1000 —ar 2:3

darkness beautiful royal huge dragon with scale wings, Magic the gathering, in spiral smoke in dark fog in background, by andrei riabovitchev, Massimo Caggese, peter mohrbacher, Omnious intricate, octane, moebius, arney freytag, gorgeous pose, ArtStation, perfect composition, dramatic lighting, dramatic shadows, orthodox symbolism, concept art, ambient, magic realism, 8k resolution, very complex hyper-maximalist overdetailed cinematic tribal darkfantasy – –stylize 1000 —ar 2:3

very complex hyper-maximalist overdetailed cinematic, gorgeous royal huge fire dragon with his beautiful queen of fire, Magic the gathering, in spiral flame in dark fog in background, Omnious intricate, octane, gorgeous pose, ArtStation, perfect composition, dramatic lighting, dramatic shadows, orthodox symbolism, concept art, ambient, magic realism, 8k resolution, tribal darkfantasy – –stylize 1000 —ar 3:2

2b nier automata, a girl in black gear with two swords, in the style of artgerm, adonna khare, anime aesthetic, c. r. w. nevinson, playful genre scenes, life-like avian illustrations, eye-catching, gray —s 300 —q 5 —ar 1:2 —upbeta —v 5

(enchantress :1.3) in spiral lightning background, glorious young woman, perfect beautiful face, realistic, full body, standing on ground, circuit board, in intricate clothing, elegant pose, fantasy, illustration, artstation, very complex hyper-maximalist overdetailed cinematic tribal darkfantasy, Detailed Face, Epic-Moody Woods in the Background, 8k resolution, Ultra-detailed Quality 3D Octane Render, photorealistic concept art, Sharp Focus, Perfect Composition, evil smile, crazy eyes, perfect hands, perfect eyes, perfect lips, (intense shadows), (intense lighting), wallpaper, HDR, high quality, high-definition

Highest quality photo God of Death, She wears a tight-fitting black leather outfit, the collar and sleeves of which are trimmed with the fur of an unknown beast from the Underworld. Has a weakness for various kinds of voodoo jewelry. Loves massive rings. In the left ear is a silver earring. His face, of course, is the most beautiful, big eyes, white skin and an unusual hairstyle terrify anyone

league of legends female character in flying dress, in the style of dark bronze and teal, futurist mechanical precision, richly detailed genre paintings, kintsugi, sleek, trompe-l'œil illusionistic detail, infinity nets, captivating cityscapes —ar 1:2 —v 5

very complex hyper-maximalist overdetailed cinematic tribal darkfantasy young beautiful woman Queen of the fire standing on ground in spiral tongue of flame background, glorious, full body, in intricate clothing, perfect and beautiful face, elegant pose, perfect composition, realistic, circuit board, fantasy, illustration, artstation, trial dark fantasy, photorealistic concept art, intense shadows, intense lighting :: 8k resolution, ultra-detailed quality 3D octane render, sharp focus, wallpaper, HDR, high quality, high-definition stylize 1000 —ar 2:3

very complex hyper-maximalist overdetailed cinematic forest deity, floral, long hair, Magic the gathering, in giant ancient tree background, gorgeous pose, by MountainDog Studios, Unreal Engine, intense lighting, intense shadows, orthodox symbolism, ambient, realism, orthodox symbolism, ambient occlusion, emotional, 8k resolution —ar 2:3

very complex hyper-maximalist overdetailed cinematic (character of video game 1:3) floral, forest deity, long hair, minimum clothing, Magic the gathering, clouds of leaves and wind, in spiral of lians in giant ancient tree background, Omnious intricate, gorgeous pose, ArtStation, Unreal Engine, intense lighting, intense shadows, orthodox symbolism, concept art, ambient, magic realism, orthodox symbolism, ambient occlusion, volumetric lighting, emotional, 8k resolution, tribal darkfantasy —ar 3:2

beautiful forest deity woman :: long hair :: pale skin :: in giant ancient tree background :: by MountainDog Studios :: Face detailed :: Character design :: model sheet :: clip art style :: 3D render :: Digital 3D :: Unreal engine :: VFX :: Cinematic lighting :: Isometric :: Low-poly :: Made in blender :: ultra realistic :: 8k :: photo realistic :: cinematic —ar 2:3 —s 1000 —chaos 100 —q 2

a three different metahuman woman coming to dark city street, in the style of full body, intricate costumes, canon eos 5d mark iv, 32k uhd, gemstone, superhero subjects

a beautiful dmg female with two swords, in the style of robotic expressionism, dark gold and dark cyan, futuristic contraptions, alois arnegger, high-angle, xu beihong, graceful poses, nusch éluard —ar 1:2 —v 5

a stuning interpretation of a womangazelle, sitting on a massive scale luxury couch, in the style of liquid shiny metal and transparent crystal, beautifully lit, artgerm, dynamic and action-packed scenes, exquisite brushwork, stripcore, crystalpunk, blink-and-you-miss-it detail, stunning concept art by: Alberto Vargas, Boris Vallejo

woman queen of spiders eledrae by taijen 3, in the style of boris vallejo, dark diamond and gold, polished metamorphosis, trompe-l'œil illusionistic detail, contemporary spider-woman, large-scale brushstrokes, stripcore —ar 1:2 —v 5 —s 300 —q 5 —upbeta —v 5

female character, in the style of robotic expressionism, dark bronze and white, interlacing artifacts, helene knoop, eye-catching detail, layered veneer panels, metallic rotation —ar 9:16 —v 5 photo taken by a photography genius, dancer with feathers and jewelry at night on the beach by the fire in the style of Emmanuel Lubezki and Antonio J. Manzanedo and Alberto Vargas and Mark Simonetti, realistic depiction of light, luminous pointillism, daz3d, the stars art group (xing xing), sultan mohammed, burned/charred —style expressive —ar 804:1344 —upanime —niji 5 —s 250 —v 5

the little girl is dancing on fire and with fire on her face, daz3d, persian miniature, made of crystals, confetti-like dots, i can't believe how beautiful this is, commission for

a woman with an axe sitting next to the fire, in the style of martin stranka, dance, backlight, stock photo, balinese art

venice in a carnival picture 3, in the style of fantastical compositions, colorful, eye-catching compositions, symmetrical arrangements, navy and aquamarine, distinctive noses, gothic references, spiral group —style expressive —ar 804:1344 —upanime —niji 5 —s 250 —v 5

beautiful temptress cancan dancers in style vaudeville burlesque dancer on stage with feathers, shiny eyes, opulent architecture, I cant even believe it so stunning, rtx on, bright luster, glossy, in the extravagant style, full body photo, cinematic shot, photo taken by canon, photo taken by hasselblad, incredibly detailed, m!shć, llll larpen, details, professional lighting, photographic lighting, 50mm, 80mm, nḿhotography, unsplash

interpretation of deadly sins - wrath, as an amazing woman, in the style of cyberdieseldream

goddess of desire::5 Professional Macro Photography::4 detailed, extreme close-up, sharp focus, natural light, award-winning, by trompe l'oeil, attention to detail::3 blurry, dim, boring, generic, simple, plain, grainy::-2 dark atmosphere, alluring pose, scandalous pose, full body, eledrae by taijen 3, triadic colors, trompe l'œil illusionistic detail, contemporary stripcore::9 incredible masterpiece hyper detailed, photoshoot moment::10 drop shadow, polished detailed, epic background, 32k, uhd, process colors::9 in the style of Bayard Wu::9 low quality, low resolution, poorly composed, gross, messy, dull, uninteresting subject matter, minimal texture, poor focus::-2 incorrect slide distance, lack of detail::-2 simple, bland, grainy, dull blurry, uninspired, deformed, watermark, plain background, simple, poor, traditional, static, cartoonish, signature::-2 boring, ugly, poorly lit, generic personality, inconsisten style, generic::-2 incorrect dimensions, cluttered layout, unrealistic textures, simple design, limited colors, poorly executed, unrealistic shading::-2

beautifully lit, dark atmosphere, alluring pose, lace fabric, scandalous pose, full body, la perla::10 incredible intricate masterpiece, hyper detailed moment::9 drop shadow, detailed, epic background, 32k, uhd, triadic color grading::9 in the style of James jean, Brian froud, Ross Tran::9 low quality, low resolution, generic, poorly composed, gross, messy, dull, uninteresting subject matter, minimal texture, dim, poor focus::-2 incorrect slide distance, lack of detail::-2 simple, bland, grainy, dull blurry, uninspired, black and white, grainy, deformed, watermark, plain background, simple, poor, traditional, static, cartoonish, signature::-2 dull, boring, ugly, poorly lit, undeveloped concept, generic personality, inconsisten style, dim, boring, generic::-2 incorrect dimensions, cluttered layout, unrealistic textures, simple design, limited colors, poorly executed, lack of detail, unrealistic shading::-2

amfibiya::10 incredible intricate masterpiece hyper realistic full body photography colaboration between dieselholographic::9,5 triadic color, drop shadow, detailed, cyberpunk background, 32k uhd, triadic color grading::9 in the style of Tom Bagshaw::8,5 low quality, low resolution, generic, poorly composed, gross, messy, dull, uninteresting subject matter, minimal texture, dim, poor focus, incorrect slide distance, lack of detail, simple, bland, grainy, dull blurry, uninspired, black and white, grainy, deformed, watermark, plain background, simple, poor, traditional, static, cartoonish, signature, dull, boring, ugly, poorly lit, undeveloped concept, generic personality, inconsistent style, dim, boring, generic, unappetizing, incorrect dimensions, cluttered layout, unrealistic textures, simple design, limited colors, non-repeatable pattern, poorly executed, lack of detail, unrealistic shading::-2

eye level view photography of a huge greenhouse of very strange and delightful flowers, from the future::5 incredible intricate masterpiece hyper realistic photography colaboration between cyberpunk::4 triadic color, drop shadow, detailed, cyberpunk background, 32k uhd, triadic color grading::4.5 in the style of Tom Bagshaw::3 blurry, uninspired, black and white, grainy, deformed, watermark, plain background, simple, poor, traditional, static, cartoonish, signature, dull, boring, ugly, poorly lit, undeveloped concept, generic personality, inconsistent style, dim, boring, generic, unappetizing, incorrect dimensions, cluttered layout, low-quality, unrealistic textures, simple design, limited colors, non-repeatable pattern, poorly executed, lack of detail, unrealistic shading::-2

a baroque portrait of a person made entirely out of feathers::5 incredible intricate masterpiece hyper realistic mega art::4 in the style of Tom Bagshaw::3 low quality, low resolution, generic, poorly composed, gross, messy, dull, uninteresting subject matter, minimal texture, dim, poor focus, incorrect slide distance, lack of detail, simple, bland, grainy, dull blurry, uninspired, black and white, grainy, deformed, watermark, plain background, simple, poor, traditional, static, cartoonish, signature, dull, boring, ugly, poorly lit, undeveloped concept, generic personality, inconsistent style, dim, boring, generic, unappetizing, incorrect dimensions, cluttered layout, unrealistic textures, simple design, limited colors, non-repeatable pattern, poorly executed, lack of detail, unrealistic shading::-2

a Cecaelia with a lot of light falling to her, in the style of dark purple and orange, demon stripcore, damned witchcraft, evilcore, luminosity of water, fallingcore, hyper realistic and hyper detailed, stunning composition, hyper emotional, epic cinematic lighting, 32k UHD resolution, made by daz3d,

DamShelma

Hope masterpiece of a damned mermaid surrounded by lots of tiny glowing fighting fish, Damned Shelma, luxcore, dark azure and white crystal, luminosity of water, solarpunk, 5d, galaxy dimension, hyper high resolution, made by daz3d, 32k UHD resolution

twilight star mermaid on dark sea, in the style of concept art, realistic brushwork, Damned Shelma, capturing the essence of this iconic character, hyper realistic and hyper detailed, stunning composition, hyper emotional, epic cinematic lighting, 32k UHD resolution, shot on Hasselblad H6D 400c Multi shot, Mitakon Speedmaster 65mm f 1.4 XCD

a anthropomorphic furry dragoness, villainess queen, luxury modern outfit, wags her hips in the crystal hall, composition evoke a sense of admiration, dark and brooding designer daz3d, strong sense of realism, dark kingcore, realistic and detailed, emotional, epic dramatic lighting, 32k UHD resolution

ultra realistic photograph of a stunning anthropomorphic femdragon beautiful gorgeous, in swimwear, lies on the water surface of the lake, stunning composition evoke a sense of admiration, hyper realistic and hyper detailed, hyper emotional, epic cinematic lighting, 32k UHD resolution, shot on Hasselblad H6D 400c Multi shot, Mitakon Speedmaster 35mm f 1.2 XCD —style expressive —ar 1:2 —upanime —niji 5 —q 3

photoshoot top angle action pose, stunning barbie girl character in black lace spider webs, surrounded by crawling demons and skull and swirling bats, emerging from swirling black fog, on the walk as a model, ultra stunning lighting, swirling black smoke and bats, stunning fashion show, essentials moments, mystery and sparks, mystical dream by DamShelma

low angle action pose, stunning diesel girl character in chrome-plated metal chains surrounded by crawling vines and holograms and swirling

64

vines emerging from swirling black fog on the cat walk as a model, ultra stunning lighting, swirling black smoke and bats, stunning fashion show, style, beautifully color coded, unreal render, iconic character, hyper realistic and hyper detailed, stunning composition, emotional, cinematic lighting, 32k UHD resolution, made by daz3d, DamShelma —style expressive —ar 1:2 —upanime —niji 5 —s 300 —q 3

Video Game Characters

Volibear, a bear with a cool design, the maniac bear in the style of dragoncore, luminous brushwork, dark white and azure, 32k uhd, detailed character design, brushwork mastery, cypherpunk, gigantic scale, james paick, frozen movement, michael malm, high resolution —s 300 —q 5 —ar 10:19 —upbeta —v 5

Death Prophet Champion from Dota2, by Arthur Palmeira

the game 'worshipers' introduces an unnamed animal called wolverine to the trailer, in the style of wollensak 127mm f/4.7 ektar, fantastical scenes, distinctive noses, brutal action, white and gold, close-up intensity

Marvel Comics Style, My little pony on a dark background, evil laugh, villainpunk portraiture, oil paint, iridescence, shiny latex rubber, cyberpunk, atompunk, volumetric light, pulp illustration, photorealism, raking light, cinematic lighting, backlit —niji 5 —style expressive —ar 9:16 —v 5 —q 5 —upbeta

brutal man king of fire in spiral flame, fog, mist background glorious , perfect face, realistic, full body, standing on ground, circuit board, in intricate clothing, fantasy, illustration, artstation, very complex hyper-maximalist overdetailed cinematic tribal darkfantasy, 8k resolution, Ultra-detailed Quality 3D Octane Render, photorealistic concept art, Sharp Focus, Perfect Composition, intense shadows, intense lighting, wallpaper, HDR, high quality, high-definition —stylize 1000 —ar 2:3

Capture an extraordinary image of a stunning cyborg with translucent, glowing body parts as she gracefully dances under a starlit sky. Her flowing, iridescent attire enhances the ethereal beauty of her movements.Full body portrait. Use a Hasselblad H4D 200MS Digital Camera, Mitakon Speedmaster 300mm f/8 XCD, ISO 100, 1/250 second

very complex hyper-maximalist overdetailed cinematic (character of video game 1:3) royal, darkness, long windblown hair and cloth, Magic the gathering, vibrant contrast, clouds of toxic fumes, smoke, in spiral of ghost in huge dark castle background, by Massimo Caggese, Omnious intricate, octane, moebius, gorgeous pose, ArtStation, Unreal Engine, dramatic lighting, dramatic shadows, orthodox symbolism, concept art, ambient, magic realism, orthodox symbolism, ambient occlusion, volumetric lighting, emotional, 8k resolution, tribal darkfantasy

a Deathwing on fire with flames rising above the city, in the style of zbrush, referential painting, spiky mounds, dark bronze and red, meticulous detail, crowcore, exaggerated expressions, stunning art by Bayard Wu

heavenly beautiful royal very big dragon with long red windblown hair and scale wings, Magic the gathering, pale skin vibrant high contrast in spiral smoke in gold fog light in background, by andrei riabovitchev, tomasz alen kopera,moleksandra shchaslyva, peter mohrbacher, Omnious intricate, octane, moebius, arney freytag, gorgeous pose, ArtStation, dramatic lighting, dramatic shadows, orthodox symbolism, ambient, magic realism, tribal darkfantasy

(character of video game 1:3) :: royal, darkness, long windblown hair and cloth, Magic the gathering, vibrant contrast, clouds of toxic fumes, smoke, in spiral of ghost in huge dark castle background, , gorgeous pose :: by Massimo Caggese, Omnious intricate, ArtStation :: dramatic shadows, orthodox symbolism, ambient, orthodox symbolism, ambient occlusion, emotional, tribal darkfantasy wallpaper :: Ultra-detailed Quality 3D :: 3d render octane :: Unreal engine :: VFX :: Cinematic lighting :: Isometric :: Made in blender :: ultra realistic :: 8k :: cinematic —s 300 —ar 9:16 —q 2

(character of video game 1:3) :: royal, darkness, long windblown hair and cloth, Magic the gathering, vibrant contrast, clouds of toxic fumes, smoke, in spiral of ghost in huge dark castle background, gorgeous pose :: portrait::-1 by Massimo Caggese, Omnious intricate, ArtStation :: dramatic shadows, orthodox symbolism, ambient, orthodox symbolism, ambient occlusion, emotional, tribal darkfantasy :: wallpaper :: Ultra-detailed Quality 3D :: 3d render octane :: Unreal engine :: VFX :: Cinematic lighting :: Isometric :: Made in blender :: ultra realistic :: 8k :: cinematic —s 300 —ar 9:16 —q 2

(character of video game 1:3)::2 royal, darkness, long windblown hair and cloth, Magic the gathering, vibrant contrast, clouds of toxic fumes, smoke, in spiral of ghost in huge dark castle background, gorgeous pose :: portrait::1 by Massimo Caggese, Omnious intricate, ArtStation :: dramatic shadows, orthodox symbolism, ambient, orthodox symbolism, ambient occlusion, emotional, tribal darkfantasy :: wallpaper :: Ultra-detailed Quality 3D :: 3d render octane :: Unreal engine :: VFX :: Cinematic lighting :: Isometric :: Made in blender :: ultra realistic :: 8k :: cinematic —s 300 —ar 9:16 —q 2

Cyberpunk anthropomorphic targarian in glittering clothes, hyper-realistic and hyper-detailed, in the rays of the sun, stunning composition, hyper-emotional, epic cinematic lighting, 8k resolution, shot on Hasselblad H6D-400c Multi-shot, Mitakon Speedmaster 65mm f/1.4 XCD

(character of video game 1:3) royal, darkness, long windblown hair and cloth, Magic the gathering, vibrant contrast, clouds of toxic fumes, smoke, in spiral of ghost in huge dark castle background, , gorgeous pose :: by

Massimo Caggese, Omnious intricate, ArtStation, dramatic shadows, orthodox symbolism, ambient, orthodox symbolism, ambient occlusion, emotional, tribal darkfantasy wallpaper :: Ultra-detailed Quality 3D :: 3d render octane :: Unreal engine :: VFX :: Cinematic lighting :: Isometric :: Made in blender :: ultra realistic :: 8k :: cinematic —s 300 —ar 9:16 —q 2.

(game character 1:3)::2 royal, darkness, Magic the gathering, vibrant contrast, in spiral of ghost in huge dark castle background, gorgeous pose :: portrait::-2 Omnious intricate, ArtStation :: dramatic shadows, orthodox symbolism, ambient, orthodox symbolism, ambient occlusion, emotional, tribal darkfantasy

side view of intricate detailed, game character eternal goddes detailed green eyes, very detailed, dim, photo, ultra-realistic, photorealistic, hyper detailed, (shot on Hasselblad H4D 200MS, HC 3.2/150N, 35mm) photography by Irving Penn and Annie Leibovitz, retouched by Pratik Naik —q 5 —ar 9:16 —seed 2127255799

Full body portrait of game character, eternal goddes, with detailed purpul eyes, shot on Hasselblad H4D 200MS Digital Camera, Mitakon Speedmaster 65mm f/1.4 XCD, Fresnel lighting —q 5 —ar 1:2

Full body portrait of game character, eternal goddes, with detailed purpul eyes, shot on Hasselblad H4D 200MS Digital Camera, Mitakon Speedmaster 65mm f/1.4 XCD, in the style of Dragon Age, Fresnel lighting —q 5 —ar 1:2

Full body portrait of game character, goddes, with detailed eyes, shot on Hasselblad H4D 200MS Digital Camera, Mitakon Speedmaster 65mm f/1.4 XCD, in the style of League og Legends, Fresnel lighting —q 5 —ar 1:2

Full length photo of the game's character, Sylvanas Windrunner, she is tall and slender, wearing light leather armor and holding a bow, emerging from the black mist that is reaching for her, shot on Hasselblad H4D 200MS Digital Camera, Mitakon Speedmaster 65mm f/1.4 XCD, Diablo Style, Fresnel lighting

Full body portrait of game character, brutal god, walk motion capture, hyper detailed, shot on Hasselblad H4D 200MS Digital Camera, Mitakon Speedmaster 65mm f/1.4 XCD, Fresnel lighting —q 5 —ar 1:2 —seed

Full body portrait of game character, Hyper realistic Poison Ivy like a God flying in space, Poison Ivy flying in front of a big magical green planet, strong features, Poison Ivy like a God, Poison Ivy clothes, space color green, neon green, glow in the dark green colors, hyper detailed, shot on Hasselblad H4D 200MS Digital Camera, Mitakon Speedmaster 65mm f/1.4 XCD, Fresnel lighting —q 5 —ar 1:2

Full body portrait of movie character, Hyper realistic Rick Sanchez and Morty like a God flying in space Rick Sanchez and Morty flying in front of a big magical planet, strong features, Rick Sanchez and Morty like a Gods, Rick Sanchez and Morty clothes, neon space glow in the dark colors, hyper detailed, shot on Hasselblad H4D 200MS Digital Camera, Mitakon Speedmaster 65mm f/1.4 XCD, Galaxy, Dimensional effect, Fresnel lighting —q 5 —ar 1:2 —s 1000

Full body portrait of game character, eternal goddes, with detailed purpul eyes, shot on Hasselblad H4D 200MS Digital Camera, Mitakon Speedmaster 65mm f/1.4 XCD, Fresnel lighting —q 5 —ar 7:13 —s 750

Hyper Detailed Motion Capture Of Casting Massive Spell of Large Scale Coven, Witchcraft, Blocksberg on Background, shot on Hasselblad H4D 200MS Digital Camera, Mitakon Speedmaster 300mm f/5.6 XCD, Dark Aesthetic, Ember Light, Intricate, Light Pollution, Epic Light —q 5 —ar 2:3

Full body portrait of game character, adorably gorgeous goddes, with eyes hyperdetailed, walk motion capture, hyper detailed, in Dishonored Style, Fresnel lighting —q 5 —ar 1:2 —v 5

A stunning watercolor impressionist painting of Plague doctor, depicting the superhero in full body form. The painting is rendered in HDR, DTM, full HD, and 8K resolution, with ultra-detailed brushwork that captures every nuance and detail of the character's iconic suit and features. The painting is created by master artists such as Artgerm, Yoshitaka Amano, or Stefan Gesell, who are known for their realism and superb skills in professional color grading. The colors are vibrant and dynamic, with soft shadows and no contrast, creating a dreamlike atmosphere that draws the viewer in. The painting is rendered with clean and sharp focus, reminiscent of film photography, adding to the timeless quality of the work. The overall effect is a breathtaking piece of art that captures the spirit and energy of Plague doctor in a unique and captivating way.A stunning watercolor impressionist painting of Plague doctor, with vibrant and dynamic colors, ultra-detailed brushwork, and clean, sharp focus, reminiscent of film photography.

Beautiful Women

eye view of a metahuman woman coming to street, in the style of attention to gloss texture, superherocore, side view, ornamental details and embellishments, detailed facial features, colorful

artistic photography of a beautiful bachata dancer in crazy moving in the gigantic city fountain, tight silky bachata outfit, wild wet hair, hourglass figure body, luminism, bar lighting, maximalist, by John William Waterhouse, polished and blink

a stunning interpretation of a beautiful woman matador, red muleta in hands, twisted corrida, tiny outfits, highly detailed and intricate, hypermaximalist, ornate, luxury, ominous, haunting, matte painting, atmospheric, cinematic, volumetric lighting, Paul Bonner, Frank Frazetta, Brian froud, ross tran

a stunning beauty Ysera in woman body, wearing luxury swimwear, lies on the water surface, queencore, stunning composition evoke a sense of admiration, hyper realistic and hyper detailed, epic cinematic lighting, 32k UHD resolution, shot on Hasselblad H6D 400c Multi shot, Mitakon Speedmaster 35mm f1.4 XCD

stunning photography of a magnificent girl in the depths of the night ether party of the adult world, sultre elegance, highly intricate, highly detailed, vibrant colors, volumetric lighting, cinematic, photorealism, photo realistic, hard focus, smooth, depth of field, in the style of Saul Bass, photo taken by a Hasselblad, 85mm lens, f/1. 4 aperture, 1/500 shutter speed, ISO 100 film, RAW photo, UHD, 32k

masterpiece, stunning full body portrait of a gorgeous lady in outfit of crystals swarovski, sultre elegance, in white marble hall, in the style of a Swarovski, highly intricate, highly detailed, cinematic, hyperrealism, photorealism, photo realistic, vibrant colors, volumetric lighting, by Joyce Ballantyne Brand, David Klein, Roberto Cavalli, Saul Bass, retouched by Pratik Naik, photo taken by a Sony Alpha 1 , 85mm lens, f/1. 4 aperture, 1/500 shutter speed, ISO 100 film, UHD, HDH, HDR, 8k, 16k, 32k —style expressive —ar 9:16 —upanime —niji 5 —q 3

villainess woman with black hair in a leather jacket and beautiful silver biker jewelry, proudly sits on chopper motorcycle, focus front, rock pub in the background, cover, hyperdetailed photoshoot, luminism, Bar lighting, complex, 32k UHD resolution concept art portrait by Greg Rutkowski, Artgerm, WLOP, little fusion pojatti realistic goth, fractal isometrics details bioluminescens

amazing gothic chimera waggling their hips at the carnival parade in scandalous outfits, by daz3d

top view photography of gorgeous metawoman, white hair and red eyes, emerging from lava in shimmering fiery pool on island, intricate details, in the style of Feng Zhu, capturing the essence of this iconic character, hyper realistic and hyper detailed, stunning composition, hyper emotional, epic cinematic lighting, 32k UHD resolution, shot on Hasselblad H6D

Full body shoot of stunnig beauty russian woman, sitting on a bench on Arbat street and feeding birds with her hand, the sun's rays pass through the trees glaring on a beautiful girl, highly detailed, vibrant, 32k UHD, by magali villeneuve, artgerm, Jeremy Lipkin, Michael Garmash, Rob Rey

dancer with feathers and jewelry at night on the beach by the fire in the style of magali villeneuve, eve ventrue, realistic depiction of light, luminous pointillism, daz3d, sultan mohammed, burned/charred

(beautiful woman, dancing flamenco)::4 intricate giant earrings, black hair, very long dress::3 huge shawl, bata de cola, frills and flounces, red-black palette :: Mudéjar style, Romanesque architecture in background, dancing pose :: portrait::-2 passion, grace, emotional, epic composition, tribal darkfantasy, dramatic shadows :: by Fabian Perez

an image of a blue dress in the dark, in the style of detailed character design, digital airbrushing, dark white and light aquamarine, 8k resolution, intricate lines, rococo whimsy, glowing colors

a female character with long white hair in armor, in the style of vibrant realism, emerald and bronze, changelingcore, red and gold, realist detail, light crimson and green, undefined anatomy

gorgeous woman created from diamond, silk, diamonds, gems, sparkling dots, in crystal cave background, style Darek Zabrocki, magic realism, gradient colors, cinematic lighting, bokeh, Ultra-detailed Quality 3D, 3d render octane, Unreal engine, VFX, Isometric, Made in blender, 8k, cinematic, ultrahd, wallpaper —no closeup portrait —s 1000 —ar 1:2

smiling witch, stuning action scene of vengeance, eledrae by taijen 3, in the style of Alberto Vargas, polished metamorphosis, trompe l'œil illusionistic detail, stripcore, dream, otherworldly, mystical realism, unique, ultra-detailed, abstract but representational, Adobe Photoshop, inspired, artistic, award-winning

woman::5 Professional Architecture Render::4 photorealistic, 3D rendering, high-quality, detailed, accurate representation, 3D Studio Max, V-Ray,
professional, corporate, award-winning, glibatree style, realistic materials,
accurate dimensions, multiple angles, perspective views::3 deformed, abstract,
unrealistic materials, incorrect dimensions, flat views::-2

woman::5 Beautiful painting with artistic symbolism::4 brushstrokes, expressive, textured, vibrant colors, traditional medium, hand-painted, impressionistic style, high-quality canvas, limited edition, oil paint, palette knife,
windsor & newton oil paints, award-winning, glibatree style::3 signature,
deformed::-2

Moulin Rouge in the style of Emmanuel Lubezki and Antonio J. Manzanedo and
Alberto Vargas and Mark Simonetti, in golden light, a scene of exotic realism,
smooth and shiny, a girl in a scarlet suit is posing in a red room, in the style of
hyper realistic oil, asian inspired, light silver and light bronze, illustration,
latex/glossy, glamorous hollywood portraits, detailed character illustrations,
i cant believe it stunning, richest jewele ornate, art nouveau, symmetrical,
transparant blue jewelry, hypermaximalist, elegant, vintage, hyper realistic,
super detailed

fullbody photoshoot of Moulin Rouge character a real gorgeous villian woman
with snow white hair, red lips, a lush hourglass figure, in black polishing
latex mini, intricate detailed in richest bejeweled, background moulin rouge,
dramatic lighting, hyper realistic, 8k cinematic, UHD, 1080p, HQ —niji 5 —q
2 —style expressive —ar 704:1344 —s 500

woman::5 Professional Impressionistic Painting, swirling brushstrokes, impasto techniques::4 expressive brushstrokes, thick, visible brushstrokes,
textured, vibrant colors, traditional medium, hand-painted, high-quality
canvas, limited edition, oil paint, palette knife, windsor & newton oil paints,

award-winning, glibatree style, attention to detail, dynamic compositions, unique subject matter::3 gold swirling masses, navy, colors, bright contrast::2 flat, dull colors, low-quality, generic, poorly composed, uninteresting subject matter, lack of detail, smooth brushstrokes, minimal texture::-2

woman::5 Fiberoptic neuron design on a black background::4 neon colors, cyan, white, purple, beautiful, intricut, stylized, ornate, glowing, magical, mystical, electricity, Maya Rending Software, gorgeous design::3 gross, messy, dull, dim::-2

character::5 Professional Impressionistic Painting, swirling brushstrokes, impasto techniques::4 expressive brushstrokes, thick, visible brushstrokes, textured, vibrant colors, traditional medium, hand-painted, high-quality canvas, limited edition, oil paint, palette knife, windsor & newton oil paints, award-winning, glibatree style, attention to detail, dynamic compositions, unique subject matter::3 gold swirling masses, navy, colors, bright contrast::2 flat, dull colors, low-quality, generic, poorly composed, uninteresting subject matter, lack of detail, smooth brushstrokes, minimal texture::-2

Hyper detailed Full body portrait of passionate woman in hyper provocate dress, flirts actively::5 Whimsical character design::4 Tags: creative, expressive, detailed, colorful, stylized anatomy, high-quality, digital art, 3D rendering, stylized, unique, award-winning, Adobe Photoshop, 3D Studio Max, V-Ray, playful, fantastical::2 plain background, simple, deformed::-2

she is a gorgeous woman coming out of a volcano and created out of lava, active volcano on background, concept by Emmanuel Lubezki and Antonio J. Manzanedo and Alberto Vargas and Vladimir Matyukhin —ar 800:1600 —v 5.1 —s 1000 **she is a gorgeous woman coming out of volcano and created out of lava, by Vladimir Matyukhin —ar 800:1600 —v 5.1 —style raw —s 300 —v 5

Hyper detailed Full body portrait of passionate woman in hyper provocate dress, flirts::5 Realistic Landscape Painting::4 brushstrokes, expressive, textured, detailed, accurate representation of nature, natural tones, traditional medium, oil paint, high-quality canvas, limited edition, award-winning, glibatree style::3 signature, dull, boring, ugly, abstract::-2

Portrait of passionate woman in hyper provocate extreme mini dress, flirts::5 Professional Macro Photography::4 detailed, extreme close-up, sharp focus, natural light, Canon EOS 5D Mark IV DSLR, f/8 aperture, 1/250 second shutter speed, ISO 100, high-quality, award-winning, by Artificial Nightmares, attention to detail::3 blurry, dim, boring, generic, simple, plain, grainy::-2 —q 5 —ar 1:2

Full height portrait beautifull Lady Godiva (fiend), with a huge snow-white braid, mini intricate dress, riding on massivescale black horse, along the steampunk street, intricate details, highly details, full body shot, (Gothic), smooth, sharp focus! Concept art by: Ruan Jia, Ilya Kuvshinov, Alphonse Mucha and Ross Draws. —ar 1:2 —q 5 —s 1000 —v 5

Stunning low angle action pose::5 stunning goth girl character in black lace spider webs::4 surrounded by crawling demons and swirling bats, emerging from swirling black fog on the cat walk as a model, hyper detailed::3 ultra stunning lighting, swirling black smoke, beautiful alluring nightwear, gorgeous female, hourglass figure, beautifully lit, dark atmosphere, alluring pose, sheer fabric, scandalous pose, full body, stunning Concept art by: Ruan JIA, Ilya Kuvshinov, Antonio J. Manzanedo, Alphonce Mucha and Ross Draws, beautifully color - coded, unreal render::4 —ar 7:13 —upbeta —q 5 —s 1000 —seed 4173587073 —v 5

Full body portrait of Luxurious woman in provocate transparent dress flirts actively::5 Whimsical character design::4 Tags: creative, expressive, detailed, colorful, stylized anatomy, high-quality, digital art, 3D rendering, stylized, unique, award-winning, Adobe Photoshop, 3D Studio Max, V-Ray, playful, fantastical, by Artificial Nightmares::2 plain background, simple, deformed::-2

Stunning action pose::10 Elsa in a revealing intricate nightwear::10 goes in ice castle::8 hyper detailed::9 ultra stunning lighting, swirling blue smoke, beautiful alluring outfit, gorgeous female, hourglass figure, beautifully lit, dark atmosphere, alluring pose, sheer fabric, scandalous pose, full body, 4D dimension, Stunning Concept art by: Stanley Artgerm, Darek Zabrocki, and Ross Draws, beautifully color - coded, unreal render::9 —s 300 —upbeta —q 5 —ar 1:2 —v 5

Queen of Blades, Sarah Louise Kerrigan, beautiful face, her skin is mottled green and covered with a shiny protective shell, her eyes are bright yellow, her hair is segmented, like insect paws, shoots the fingers of the Queen of Blades are armed with retractable claws, wings consisting of elongated segmented spikes that reach the level of the knees along with other claws Kerrigan uses in close combat and wings, literally tearing the imitation of opponents apartmystical::10 dark gothic, stunning, hypermaximalist, elegant, ornate, luxury, elite, ominous, cgsociety, style of StarCraft, hyper-realistic, matte painting, enhanced::8 carved, action pose, violent, vengeful, insanely detailed and intricate, carved colorfull marble,persian rug, art nouveau architecture, by Will Murai::9 complex, cinematic lighting, dark, angry, action pose, violent, vengeful, multiverse, insanely detailed and intricate, hyper maximalist, elegant, ornate, luxury, elite, ominous, line details, golden section, visionary art, matte painting, cinematic, cgsociety, trending on artstation, beautiful highly detailed, by Blizzard Entertainment::8 —s 300 —upbeta —q 5 —ar 1:2 —v 5

Full body detailed portrait of Steamgothicwood villain woman, flowing maxi dress with lace and fringe, Layered jewelry with feathers and stones, rainbow palette::5 Professional Fabric Weave Design::4 traditional medium, hand-embroidered, unique, trendy, modern, unique, vector graphics, Adobe Illustrator, professional, corporate, scalable, award-winning, by Stanley Artgerm Lau, realistic textures, intricate detailing, multiple colors, repeatable pattern::3 deformed, unrealistic textures, simple design, limited colors, non-repeatable pattern::-2 —q 5 —ar 1:2 —upbeta —v 5 cyberfloral gothic woman —s 500 —q 5 —ar 1:2 —upbeta —v 5

Hyper detailed an epic scene, a voodoo shaman in an provocate outfit, made of the finest threads of silk, perfect ideal face, hourglass figure, her tattoo on marbled skin extra sparkles and extra iridescence in the moonlight, intricate hairstyle, stunning beautiful spell through mystical unearthly ruins, symbolizing the ritual tribe ascension, Hyper detailed, Hyper realistic, 4d, dimension, swirling galaxy fog, Dark Aesthetic, scandalous action pose, full body, alluring pose, unreal engine, galaxy, 3d octane render, Dark tribal darkfantasy, CGI, Dark Fantasy by Stanley Artgerm —upbeta —s 500 —ar 10:21 —q 5 —v 5

High angle action scene of two goddesses in space dimension is realistic and detailed::10 holographic intricate outfits::7 Hyper detailed eyes::9 skin shimmers in the moonlight, epic emotions and movements, swirling galaxy fog, aesthetic action, scandalous action, full body, hyper detail, hyper realism, 4d, dimension, unreal engine, galaxy, 3d octane rendering, CGI, dark fantasy, stuning art by Stanley Artgerm::8 —s 300 —upbeta —ar 10:21 —q 5 —v 5

Warriors

(brutal man warrior) intricate armor, intricate weapon, dark tones palette, battlefield in background::4 militant pose :: portrait::-2 rage, anger, power, emotional, epic composition, tribal darkfantasy, dramatic shadows

brutal man warrior, smile evil::4 intricate armor, intricate weapon, dark tones palette, battlefield in background, militant pose :: portrait::-4 emotional, epic composition, dramatic shadows :: trend artstation :: wallpaper, 3d render octane, VFX, Cinematic lighting, Isometric, Made in blender, 8k, cinematic —no closeup portrait —s 1000 —ar 2:3 —q 2 concept art of a warrior woman-elf gorgeous and beautiful, at the end of epicbattle in victory motion, powerfull rage of goddess, with intricate armor and weapon, forgotten battlefield on background, occlusion, epic wide shot, aerial perspective, darkfantasy, CGI, depth focus, crepuscular rays, Sunbeams, photorealistic, realistic, detailed, complicated, complicated maximalist, hyperrealistic, in the Dragon Age Style

Masterpiece fullbody photoshoot of a necromancer soldier of the future in royal armor, cyber technology, at the head of the imperial army in wining pose, holographic and diesel, inspired art by Adam Fisher

Monsters

giant monster, darkness, agressive pose :: epic emotional, rage, anger, power, tribal darkfantasy

giant sea monsters, battle, darkness, the Triassic period, deep ocean background, Magic the gathering, vibrant contrast, agressive pose :: orthodox symbolism, ambient, orthodox symbolism, ambient occlusion, epic emotional, rage, anger, power, tribal darkfantasy :: cinematic lighting, volumetric lighting, dramatic shadows :: 3D render :: digital art 3D :: unreal engine :: vfx :: cinematic :: isometric :: character design :: model sheet

twomassivescalemonsters&epicbattlepowerfull ageanger, deep sea, deepUnderwaterackground, occlusion, epic wide shot, aerial perspective, darkfantasy, League of Legends StyleSea of Theaves Style, CGI, depth focus, crepuscular rays, photorealistic, realistic, detailed, hyperrealistic, complicated, complicated maximalist —ar 2:1 —q 2 —s 1000

a very detailed the animal black panther in intricate made of liquid metal armor, in the style of fluid dynamic brushwork, dark black and black, ue5, sharp angles, close - up, changelingcore —ar 128:192 —ar 1:2 —v 5 —s 300

—q 5 —upbeta

Fantasy Characters

incredible depiction of a anthropomorphic eagle-owl shaman, ancient and old, ornate trinkets, elaborate, tribal, beautiful, highly detailed and intricate, hypermaximalist, ornate, luxury, ominous, smoke, atmospheric desert, haunting, matte painting, cinematic, cgsociety, Antonio J. Manzanedo, Vladimir Matyukhin, Brian froud

dracula by dwight eisner | euska, in the style of joel robison, close-up, rococo style, carnivalcore, magali villeneuve, distinctive noses, gaston lachaise —ar 1:2 —s 300 —q 3 —v 5.1

ultra detailed photograph of anthropomorphic femdragon beautiful and elegant, intricate luxury attire, siting on dragoqueen nest, stunning composition evoke a sense of admiration, hyper realistic and hyper detailed, hyper emotional, epic cinematic lighting, 32k UHD resolution, shot on Hasselblad H6D 400c Multi shot, Mitakon Speedmaster 35mm f 1.2 XCD

goat warrior wearing viking armor, beautiful, highly detailed and intricate, hypermaximalist, ornate, luxury, elite, ominous, haunting, matte painting, cinematic, cgsociety, James jean, Brian froud, ross tran

Masterpiece of a soldier of the future in royal armor, at the head of the imperial army, inspired art by Bayard Wu

Hyper detailed Brutal man in DJ headphones sitting on a rock looking down at the stunningly futuristic ruins of the city after the apocalypse::5 Character Concept Art::4 creative, expressive, detailed, colorful, stylized anatomy, digital art, 3D rendering, unique, award-winning, Adobe Photoshop, 3D Studio

Max, V-Ray, professional, glibatree style, well-developed concept, distinct personality, consistent style, by Stanley Artgerm Lau::3 deformed, simple, undeveloped concept, generic personality, inconsistent style::-2 —s 500 —q 5 —ar 1:2 —upbeta —v 5

a chemical spill mutates a mad scientist into a muscular demonic man, dark souls, castlevania. —c 2 —ar 9:16 —v 5.1 —style raw —q 2 —s 250

The Angry Princess from THIR13EN Ghosts::5 Digital Art::4 eledrae by taijen 3, in the style of boris vallejo, polished metamorphosis, trompe - l'œil illusionistic detail, large - scale brushstrokes, stripcoredream, otherworldly, surrealist techniques, unique, ultra-detailed, abstract but representational, Adobe Photoshop, inspired, artistic, award-winning, by Stanley Artgerm Lau::3 photo, dull, simple, clean, modern::-2 —s 500 —ar 9:16 —v 5 —q 5 —upbeta

a cartoon avatar with short dreadlocks, in the style of hyper-realistic atmospheres, detailed crowd scenes, cobra, american barbizon school, realistic detail, movie still, manticore

Motion apture an extraordinary image of a stunning cyborg ballerina with translucent, glowing body parts as she dancing passionately under a starlit sky, flowing, iridescent attire enhances the ethereal beauty of her movements, full body portrait::5 Futuristic Sci-Fi 3D Render::4 high-tech, science fiction, neon lighting, intriguing, imaginitive futuristic, detailed, realistic, 3D rendering, metalic, digital art, Unreal Engine 6, 3D Studio Max, V-Ray, award-winning, by Artificial Nightmares::3 deformed::-2 —s 300 —upbeta —q 5 —ar 9:21 —v 5

Nosferatu A Symphony of Horror, daz3d, by artificial nightmares

Antagonist Scar from the Lion King real handsome man by Tom Bagshaw incredible detailed shot of a magnificent dragon waking up from a thousand years of sleep, the gaze of half-open eyes driving you insane, concept art by Antonio Manzanedo

galaxy man cybergoth Indiana Jones by Vladimir Matyukhin —ar 800:1600 —v 5.1 —style raw

Mystical fox with nine tailes, in the style of Ori and the Blind Forest, epic, fantasy, intricate, hyper detailed, artstation, concept art, smooth, sharp focus, ray tracing —s 1000 —q 5 —ar 1:2 —upbeta —v 5

An amazing creature, incredibly cute appearance with a hellishly evil soul, in the style of good and evil, demonangel mythiccore, white mysticcraft, luminosity of background, fallingcore, hyper realistic and hyper detailed, stunning composition, hyper emotional, epic cinematic lighting, 32k UHD resolution, made by daz3d, DamShelma

frightening wolf, in the style of Ori and the Blind Forest, epic, fantasy, intricate, hyper detailed, artstation, concept art, smooth, sharp focus, ray tracing —s 300 —q 5 —ar 1:2 —upbeta —v 5

Appa is Avatar Aangs sky bison, white and azure, lots of long fur, luminosity of background, fallingcore, hyper realistic and hyper detailed, stunning composition, hyper emotional, epic cinematic lighting, 32k UHD resolution, made by daz3d, DamShelma —ar 1:2 —upanime —niji 5 —s 500 —q 3

neuro space cowboy riding a galaxy sky bison, inky and petrol, lots of long fur, background brightness, fullcore, risecore, hyper-realistic and hyper-detailed, stunning composition, hyper-emotional, epic cinematic lighting, 32k UHD resolution, made by daz3d, DamShelma —ar 16:9 —upanime —niji 5 —s 300 —q 3

a creature in a blackindigo lace outfit with glow cyborg eyes, artificial nightmares, fantasy personage portrait, a full body portrait, unbelievable fantasy art, by Tim Burton

Full body portrait of Rick Sanchez, in the style of Don't Starve, epic, fantasy, intricate, hyper detailed, artstation, concept art, smooth, sharp focus, ray tracing —s 300 —q 5 —ar 1:2 —upbeta —v 5

Epic wide angle view, stunning dangerous Siren mermaid with very long Betta splendens intricate tail, hovering in the deep underwater space, surrounded by water creatures, stunning perfect properties, perfect symmetric, in the style of Ori and the blind forest::10 —s 300 —q 5 —ar 1:2 —upbeta —v 5

Threefaced Cerberus guarding the exit from the realm of the dead in hades::10 anger, powerfull, rage::10 occlusion, epic wide shot, aerial perspective, dark-fantasy, Diablo Style, CGI, depth focus, dark lighting, detailed, complicated, stunning composition, complicated maximalist, by Antonio J. Manzanedo::8 —s 700 —upbeta —ar 10:21 —q 5

Cerber powerfull, rage, anger, occlusion, epic wide shot, darkfantasy, CGI, depth focus, dark lighting, realistic, detailed, complicated, stunning composition, complicated maximalist, occlusion, epic wide shot, darkfantasy, Cinematic lighting, Volumetric lighting, Epic composition, perfect composition, Photorealism, hyper detailed, Character design, Unreal Engine, Octane render, HDR, Subsurface scattering, Fresnel lighting, by Antonio J. Manzanedo::9 —s 300 —upbeta —q 5 —ar 7:13 —v 5

alice in wonderland, mad hatter the magician in a tarot card, highly detailed, half skull face, cinematic, 8 k, style by stanley artgermm, tom bagshaw, carne griffiths, hyper detailed, full of colour

Stunning action pose ::4 stunning real alchemist girl character in a revealing outfit ::10 sits on a high chair at a table in her elaborate laboratory, admiring the result of her alchemical manipulations::6 hyper detailed ::6 ultra stunning lighting, rainbow smoke, beautiful alluring nightwear, gorgeous female, hourglass figure, beautifully lit, dark atmosphere, alluring pose, sheer fabric, scandalous pose, full body, stunning Concept art by: Ruan JIA, Ilya Kuvshinov, Antonio J. Manzanedo, Alphonce Mucha and Ross Draws, beautifully color - coded, unreal render ::5

(Wooden boards overgrown with moss entwined along the edge of intricate and various leaves and twigs)::5 Whimsical character design::4 Tags: creative, expressive, detailed, colorful, stylized anatomy, high-quality, digital art, 3D rendering, stylized, unique, award-winning, Adobe Photoshop, 3D Studio Max, V-Ray, playful, fantastical::2 plain background, simple, deformed::-2

a fantastical creature that blends the best of human, animal, and mythical traits

photoart of a leprechaun as a brutal and athletic red-haired man, 32k, style expressive, high quality, expressive, epic scene, cinematic, UHD, concept by Artificial Nightmares —niji 5 —style expressive —ar 800:1600 —upanime —s 500

Hyper detailed Full body portrait of passionate woman in hyper provocate dress, flirts actively::5 Whimsical character design::4 Tags: creative, expressive, detailed, colorful, stylized anatomy, high-quality, digital art, 3D rendering, stylized, unique, award-winning, Adobe Photoshop, 3D Studio Max, V-Ray, playful, fantastical::2 plain background, simple, deformed::-2

anthropomorphic Targarian in glittering clothes::5 Professional Macro Photography::4 detailed, extreme close-up, sharp focus, natural light, Canon EOS 5D Mark IV DSLR, f/8 aperture, 1/250 second shutter speed, ISO 100, high-quality, award-winning, glibatree style, attention to detail::3 blurry, dim, boring, generic, simple, plain, grainy::-2

Hyper detailed anthropomorphic Targarian in glittering clothesornate: ::5

High Resolution Photograph with hyperornate details::4 intricate design, gold and metallic decorations, beautiful accents, Canon EOS 5D Mark IV DSLR, f/8, ISO 100, 1/250 second, rim lighting, maximum detail, flattering designs, ambitious, artistic, unknown style::3 simple, bland, grainy, dull::-2

Hyper detailed anthropomorphic Targarian in glittering::5 Character Concept Art::4 creative, expressive, detailed, colorful, stylized anatomy, digital art, 3D rendering, unique, award-winning, Adobe Photoshop, 3D Studio Max, V-Ray, professional, glibatree style, well-developed concept, distinct personality, consistent style::3 deformed, simple, undeveloped concept, generic personality, inconsistent style::-2

Hyper detailed portrait of a terrifying werewolf with Fearsome detailed fangs and frightening detailed eyes, long fur, Cinematic lighting, Volumetric lighting, Epic composition, perfect composition, Photorealism, Bokeh blur, hyper detailed, Character design, Unreal Engine, Octane render, HDR, Subsurface scattering, shot on Hasselblad H4D 200MS Digital Camera, Mitakon Speedmaster 65mm f/1.4 XCD, Fresnel lighting —q 5 —ar 1:2 —upbeta —v 5

dragon by Antonio J. Manzanedo —q 5 —ar 1:2 —v 5

dragon by Antonio J. Manzanedo —q 5 —ar 1:2 —upbeta —v 5

Ursula from Disney real beautiful and elegance woman by Art Station —q2 —1:2 —v 5

Glam metal Ishtar wearing King Tut's gold shamrock mask , art by Antonio J. Manzanedo, dynamic pose, stunning dance, atmospheric lighting, magical —q 2 —ar 10:21 —v 5

werewolf by Cynthia Sheppard —q 5 —ar 1:2 —upbeta —v 5

broken scarlet dress, stunningly beautifull, very long, intricate details, sinking, deep black water in background, contrast lighting, style by world of warcraft cinematic, Ultra-detailed Quality 3D, 3d render octane, 8k, cinematic, wallpaper —s 1000 —ar 2:1 —q 2

elegancegorgeousqueenazshara&readingspellemotionalintencepaciongrace, eyes+yellow+glowing, longwhitehair&sparkling, verylongreddressintricate&flowing, neoclassicarchitectureackground, Moonbeamslight, starlighting, epic composition, intricate surface detail, romangoddess-style, full body portrait, Ethereal Lighting, HSL, photorealistic, 8k, 1080p, sharp focus, depth focus, contemporary realism, hyperrealistic, ultra-quality, complicated, award winning art style —ar 2:3 —q 2 —s 1000

full body&move&dancesposeslow motion, anatomical, little&creepy&girlwizard, cloakdarkleatherintricate pattern, toxicspell&bottle&littleconjurehand, dark&moody&universeackground, insanely, detailed, bloom, highest quality, digital art, concept art, 8k, high sharpness, detailed pupils, digital design, detailed face and eyes, Masterpiece, best quality, highly detailed photo, 8k, photorealistic, sharp, perfect body, realistic, intricate shadow, 3d, style by Chao Teng Zhao —ar 2:3 —q 2 —s 1000

massivescale&warriors&woman&elf&gorgeous&beautifulepicbattle, run/poseslow motion, powerfull agegoddes, intricate&armor&weapon, forgotten/-battlefield, firewallackground, occlusion, epic wide shot, aerial perspective, darkfantasy, CGI, depth focus, crepuscular rays, Sunbeams, photorealistic, realistic, detailed, complicated, complicated maximalist, hyperrealistic, in the Dragon Age Style —ar 3:2 —q 2

((((full body Portrait~UrsuladisneycharacterRealBeautifulGorgeousEleganceWoman)+(verywhitehair.redlips.aristocraticface)+(longblackdress.silk.Intricate Surface Detail)*(Bejeweled.Alchemy.background)))+Dramatic Lighting+Hyperrealistic+Detailed+Hyperdetailed+8k+cinematic+UHD+1080p+HQ+CGSociety) Painting by Paul Cezane —q 5 —ar 7:13 —s 1000

((Motion Capture×YzmadisneycharacterRealBeautifulEleganceWoma n)×(violethair.violetlips.blackfeatherboa))×(miniblackdress.silk.Intricate.Be-jeweled*20sackground)×Dramatic Lighting×Hyperrealistic×Detailed×Hyper-detailed×8k×cinematic×UHD×1080p+HQ×CGSociety) in the style of 20s —q 5 —ar 7:13 —s 1000

Motion-Capture~CovenCastingSuperMassiveSpell-Magic-Witchcraft-Ember Light-Lightcore-IntricateLight PollutionEpic LightUnder-Illumination BlocksbergBackground+Dramatic-Lighting+Hyperrealistic+RealisticDe-tailed+Hyperdetailed+8k+Cinematic+UHD+1080p+HQ+CGSociety+Dark Aesthetic—q 5 —ar 13:7 —s 1000

(two Egyptian princesses fighting among themselves in mini armor :1.3) in wind sands of Ancient Egypt background, glorious young woman, perfect beautiful face, realistic, (full body), elegant pose, fantasy, illustration, artsta-tion, Perfect Composition (intense shadows), (intense lighting) —ar 2:3 —q 5 —s 1000 —chaos 100

Motion capture,Overdetailed/(Pisces woman with Pisces man move in dance passion under deep ocean starlight :3)/(gorgeous pose,hyper-emotionalism,love,magnificent,Omnious intricate,royal,Magic)/in spiral of move collection all zodiacal constellations in backgroundTrending ArtStation,CGI,Perfect Composition,realistic,detailed,(intense shadows), (intense lighting) —q 5 —ar 1:2 —s 1000

**RAW Insanely detailed studio full body portrait shotphoto of intricately detailed young beautifully woman with detailed ice eyes very detaileddim light, photo, ultra-realistic, photorealistic, hyper detailed, photography shot on Leica SL2, f/5,6 ,105mm lens, photography by Irving Penn and Annie Leibovitz, and retouched by Pratik Naik —q 5 —ar 1:2

Detailed studio full body portrait shotphoto of intricately detailed young beautiful blue hair woman smirking mischievously at the camera, with mischievous detailed bright violet eyes very detaileddim light, photo, ultra-realistic, photorealistic, hyper detailed, photography shot on Leica SL2, f/5,6 ,105mm lens, photography by Irving Penn and Annie Leibovitz, and retouched by Pratik Naik —q 5 —ar 1:2

Beautiful asian woman smirking mischievously at the camera with mischievous ultradetailed bright blue eyes , very detailed, rim light, photo, rim light, ultra-realistic, photorealistic, hyper detailed, photography, shot on Leica SL2, f/5,6 ,105mm lens , photography by Irving Penn and Annie Leibovitz and retouched by Pratik Naik —q 5 —ar 1:2

full body photo of intricately detailed/ man in mask detailed_scarlet_eye: very detailed, dim, photo, ultra-realistic, photorealistic, hyper detailed, photography shot on Leica SL2, f/5,6 ,105mm lens, photography by Irving Penn and Annie Leibovitz, and retouched by Pratik Naik —q 5 —ar 1:2 —s 1000

Side-View of Intricately Detailed Beautiful Gorgeous Elegance Warrior Woman_lies in Full Growth_in intricate Mini Dress_on carpet Made of Black Panther_Full Body photo intricately_glowing_eyes_very detailed_dim_photo_ultra-realistic_photorealistic_hyper detailed_photography shot on Leica SL2, f/5,6 ,105mm lens, photography by Irving Penn and Annie Leibovitz, and retouched by Pratik Naik —q 5 —ar 16:9 —s 1000

Side-View of Intricately Detailed Beautiful Gorgeous Elegance Warrior Woman with big glowing eyes_lies in Full Growth_in jewelry Dress_on carpet Made of Black-White fur_Full Body photo intricately_very detailed_dim_photo_ultra-realistic_photorealistic_hyper detailed_photography shot on Leica SL2, f/5,6 ,105mm lens, photography by Irving Penn and Annie Leibovitz, and retouched by Pratik Naik —q 5 —ar 16:9 —s 1000

Motioncapture spacemassivescaledragonAurelionSol underdeepspacestarligh t magicinspiralofmovezodiacalconstellations Inbackground —q 5 —ar 1:2 —s

1000 —seed 2127255799

Motioncapture spacemassivescaledragonAurelionSol underdeepspacestarligh t magicinspiralofmovezodiacalconstellations Inbackground

(fabled character of fairy tale1:3) from the dark kingdom, with hyper-realistic details - hair blowing in the wind, his clothes are intricately orthodox symbolic, his large eyes are full of horror, shot on H6D-400c Multi-shot Mitakon Speedmaster 65mm f/1.4 XCD, Fresnel lighting —q 5 —ar 1:2

hyper-realistic (fabled character tale1:3) from the dark kingdom, with detailed eyes, clothes are intricately orthodox symbolic, his large eyes are full of horror, shot on Hasselblad H4D 200MS Digital Camera, Mitakon Speedmaster 65mm f/1.4 XCD, Fresnel lighting —q 5 —ar 1:2 —seed 2127255799

Hyper-realistic (goddess character 1:3) from the dark kingdom, with hyper detailed eyes, clothes are intricately symbolic, her large rainbow eyes are full of horror, shot on Hasselblad H4D 200MS Digital Camera, Mitakon Speedmaster 65mm f/1.4 XCD —q 5 —ar 1:2

Hyper realistic picture of Elsa like a God flying in space with planets floating around Elsa, flying in front of a big magical ice planet, strong features, like a God, Elsa clothes, cold space color, neon glow in the dark colors, high details —q 5 —ar 1:2

Massive scale Lion made of Fluorescent, gorgeous beautiful run, hunting, powerfull, rage, goddes, epic wide shot, darkfantasy, CGI, depth focus, shot on Hasselblad H6D-400c Multi-shot, Mitakon Speedmaster 300mm f/5,6 XCD, mood lighting —q 5 —ar 1:2

Hyper detailed mysterious spring goddess, in the forest of dreams, sweet and tender, picking spring flowers, in Bless style, realistic , cinematic, 8k resolution, shot on Hasselblad H4D 200MS Digital Camera, epic lighting, perfect composition —q 5 —ar 1:2 —v 5

Hyper detailed anthropomorphic Targarian in glittering robes, hyper-realistic and hyper-detailed, in the rain, stunning composition, hyper-emotional, epic cinematic lighting, 8k resolution, shot on Hasselblad H6D-400c Multi-shot —ar 1:2 —q 2 —v 4 —chaos 100

Hyper detailed anthropomorphic in glittering clothes, hyper-realistic and hyper-detailed, in the rain, stunning composition, hyper-emotional, epic cinematic lighting, 8k resolution, shot on Hasselblad H6D-400c Multi-shot, Mitakon Speedmaster 65mm f/1.4 XCD —ar 1:2 —q 2 —v 4 —chaos 100

Hyper detailed anthropomorphic in glittering clothes, hyper-realistic and hyper-detailed, in the rays of the sun, stunning composition, hyper-emotional, epic cinematic lighting, 8k resolution, shot on Hasselblad H6D-400c Multi-shot —ar 1:2 —q 2 —v 4 —chaos 100

Hyper detailed anthropomorphic targarian in glittering clothes, hyper-realistic and hyper-detailed, at night, stunning composition, hyper-emotional, epic cinematic lighting, 8k resolution, shot on Hasselblad H6D-400c Multi-shot, Mitakon Speedmaster 65mm f/1.4 XCD —ar 1:2 —q 2 —v 4 —chaos 100

Hyper detailed anthropomorphic in glittering clothes, hyper-realistic and hyper-detailed, at night, stunning composition, hyper-emotional, epic cinematic lighting, 8k resolution, shot on Hasselblad H6D-400c Multi-shot, Mitakon Speedmaster 65mm f/1.4 XCD —ar 1:2 —q 2 —v 4 —chaos 100

Kerberos guarding the exit from the realm of the dead in hades::10 anger, powerfull, rage::10 occlusion, epic wide shot, aerial perspective, darkfantasy, CGI, depth focus, dark lighting, detailed, complicated, stunning composition, complicated maximalist, by Antonio J. Manzanedo::9 —s 700 —upbeta —ar 10:21 —q 5

Three-faced Cerber powerfull, rage, anger, occlusion, epic wide shot, darkfantasy, CGI, depth focus, dark lighting, realistic, detailed, complicated, stunning composition, complicated maximalist, by Antonio J. Manzanedo::9 —s 300 —q 5 —ar 7:13 —v 5

Hyper-detailed Gargoyle with large wings, strong, gorgeous, incredibly beautiful, sits in stunning pose on the roof of a massive scale dark Gothic castle ::5 Character Concept Art::4 creative, expressive, detailed, colorful, stylized anatomy, digital art, 3D rendering, unique, award-winning, Adobe Photoshop, 3D Studio Max, V-Ray, professional, glibatree style, well-developed concept, distinct personality, consistent style,by Artificial Nightmares::3 deformed, simple, undeveloped concept, generic personality, inconsistent style::-2 —s 300 —upbeta —ar 10:21 —q 5 —v 5

Adorable stunning Gorgon, with snake tail, hair is moving snakes, her whole perfect hourglass figure body is covered with shiny scales, copper hands with sharp steel claws, wings with sparkling golden plumage::10 dark gothic, stunning, hypermaximalist, elegant, ornate, luxury, elite, ominous, cgsociety, style of StarCraft, hyper-realistic, matte painting, enhanced::8 carved, action pose, violent, vengeful, insanely detailed and intricate, carved colorfull marble,persian rug, art nouveau architecture, by Will Murai::9 complex, cinematic lighting, dark, angry, action pose, violent, vengeful, multiverse, insanely detailed and intricate, hyper maximalist, elegant, ornate, luxury, elite, ominous, line details, golden section, visionary art, matte painting, cinematic, cgsociety, trending on artstation, beautiful highly detailed, by Blizzard Entertainment::8 —s 300 —upbeta —ar 10:21

An epic fly scene, a girl in an provocate outfit made of the finest threads of ultraviolet, her diamond skin extra sparkles and extra shimmers in the light of a huge moon, a girl is divinely beautiful, flying like superhuman in mystically unearthly ruins, symbolizing the ritual ascent of the deity, hyper detailed, hyper realistic, 4d dimension, swirling ultramarine fog, Dark Aesthetic, scandalous action pose, full body, alluring position, Dark Fantasy by Stanley Artgerm, unreal engine, galaxy, 3d octane ranger —s 300 —upbeta —ar 10:21 —v 5

Concept art of a star wars character, a Sith, Diabolic fiend, incredibly beautiful and dangerous, with Sith lightsaber in hand, runs along the deck of a spaceship, epic emotions and movements, swirling galaxy fog, Perfect Composition, aesthetic action, scandalous action, full body, hyper realism, 5D Dimension, unreal engine, galaxy, 3d octane rendering, CGI, dark fantasy, trending on Artstation —upbeta —ar 12:24 —q 5 —v 5a

Character design, Cinderella, mist, photorealistic, octane render, unreal engine, hyper detailed, volumetric lighting, hdr::5 Professional Architecture Render::4 photorealistic, 3D rendering, high-quality, detailed, accurate representation, 3D Studio Max, V-Ray, professional, corporate, award-winning, by Stanley Artgerm Lau, realistic materials, accurate dimensions, multiple angles, perspective views::3 deformed, abstract, flat views::-2 —s 300 —upbeta —q 5 —ar 9:21 —v 5

Star Wars character, a Sith, Hyper detailed portrait of Zabrak woman Darth Maul, incredibly beautiful and dangerous, with Sith lightsaber in hand, runs along the deck of a spaceship, epic emotions and movements, galaxy fog, Perfect Composition, aesthetic, scandalous pose, full body, hyper realism, 5D Dimension, unreal engine, galaxy, 3d octane rendering, CGI, dark fantasy, by Zack Snyder —s 300 —q 5 —ar 1:2 —upbeta —v 5

macro view of the stuning magical cybersteampgems laboratory, in the center of the image is a round sophisticated marbel table with the remnants of magical cybertechnology, in the center of the table is a huge intricate bottle with galaxy magic inside, contrasting lighting, 5D dimension, unreal engine, in the style of Dont Starve, stuning concept art by Stanley Artgerm —ar 1:3 —v 5 —q 5 —upbeta

fantasy world mutants in tightly outfits, passion kissing motion, nature background, candle lighting, in the style of diablo, hyper detailed, 5d dimension, vfx, perfect properties, 8k, unreal engine 5, 3d octane render, stunning digital concept art by artgerm

Cinderella's very high crystal transparent stiletto heel, against the backdrop of the royal palace::4 3D rendering, high-quality, detailed, accurate representation, 3D Studio Max, V-Ray, professional, corporate, award-winning, byStanley Artgerm Lau, realistic materials, accurate dimensions, multiple angles::3 deformed::-2 —s 500 —q 5 —ar 1:2 —upbeta —v 5

A character from the fantasy world, in the style of dark white and light violet, intricate costumes, realistic renderings of the human form, dark cyan and gold, elegant figures, blink - and - you - miss - it detail, stylish costume design

zoomorph, character diversity, 5D dimension, hyper detailed, intricate details, Ornatrix, VFX, 4k, unreal engine 6, 4D octane render, realistic, stunning digital concept art by Artgerm

interpretation of a fractal unholy cheshire cat, on alice in wonderland forest, mystical unearthly background, evil laugh, villian portraiture, fractalcore, dynamic pose, fit-thick-build, gorgeous perfect Cheshire, in the style of realistic and hyper - detailed renderings, kawaii, zbrush, hyper - realistic oil, contoured shading

a detailed stuning interpretation of a fairy Olga Volha Piashko, sitting on a massive scale cherry blossom tree in the style of contrast fuchsia and shiny white, swirls of petals, artgerm, dynamic and action-packed scenes, exquisite brushwork, stripcore, fairycherrypunk, blink-and-you-miss-it detail, stunning concept art by: Alberto Vargas, Boris Vallejo

half-length portrait of stuning brutal guy, tarot card with intricate detailed frame around the outside, cyberpunk body, stripcore, styled in Art Nouveau, insanely detailed embellishments, high definition, concept art, digital art, vibrant, gorgeous, trending on artstation, sharp focus, studio photo, intricate details, highly detailed, by Darek Zabrocki, Adam Fisher, Ruan Jia —niji 5 —style expressive —q 2 —upanime —ar 640:1344 —s 250

horseman of the apocalypse - Hunger, in style of fog and metal, detailed face, lush environment, cinematic light, apocalypsecore, character portrait by Annie Leibovitz, retouched by Pratik Naik

gorgeous π goddess with a tiger and a panther, detailed face, on jungle throne, lush environment, cinematic light, junglecore, character portrait by Annie Leibovitz, retouched by Pratik Naik

Buildings

Top view of hyper detailed supermassive royal castle, from dark fantasy, CGI, depth focus, Volumetric Lighting, photorealistic, realistic, detailed, hyperrealistic, complicated, complicated maximalistic —q 5 —ar 1:2

Massive scale axonometry, dark horror fantasy haunted house on the edge of a dark hill, highly detailed, illustration, fantasy art, in the style of Ori and the Blind Forest, epic, fantasy, intricate, hyper detailed, artstation, concept art, smooth, sharp focus, ray tracing —q 5 —ar 1:2 —upbeta —v 5

image of a city in deep space, in the style of columns and totems, daniel f. gerhartz, atmospheric clouds, fantastical ruins, realistic hyper-detail, exotic landscapes, industrialization —ar 625:1041 —s 300 —q 5 —ar 9:20 —upbeta —v 5

gigantic victorian conservatory, inside in a wedding dance beautiful newly-weds, her huge stunningly beautiful wedding dress flowing, overcast evening atmosphere, nature details, ultra epic wide shot, cinematic lighting, by Emmanuel Lubezki and Antonio J. Manzanedo and Alberto Vargas and Vladimir Matyukhin

Landscapes and Photography

garden with incredible flowers::5 floralcore, organic design, science fiction::4 low-quality, low-resolution, generic, poorly composed, gross, messy, dull, uninteresting subject matter, minimal texture, dim, poor focus, incorrect slide distance, lack of detail, simple, bland, grainy, dull::-2

a dead old and rusty body of a robot lying in the forrest, plants and flowers grow out of the body of robot, depth of field, bokeh effect, ultra realistic, cinematography, hyper detailed, absolute realism

Hypermacro photography of Spring bright intricate flower, breaking through a blizzard, Sunbeams rays illuminates on flower, springtime is coming, in finale fantasy style, shot on Hasselblad H4D 200MS Digital Camera, Mitakon Speedmaster 300mm f/4 XCD, epic lighting —q 5 —ar 1:2 —v 5

elven city of marble, among large trees, river with a stone bridge, detailed, Lord of the Rings, beautifully detailed 8k octane rendering, post-processing, extremely hyper-detailed, intricate, epic composition, gloomy yet bright atmosphere, cinematic lighting, masterpiece, trending on artstation, highly detailed, sf

A young man. His appearance would have struck the imagination of the most superficial observer. He was over six feet tall, but seemed even taller for his extraordinary thinness. His eyes were sharp and penetrating, and his thin eagle nose gave his face an expression of lively energy and determination. The square, slightly forward jawline also spoke of a resolute character. His hands were perpetually stained with ink and chemicals, but he had the ability to handle objects with surprising delicacy.He led a quiet, measured life and was usually true to his habits. Rarely did he go to bed after ten o'clock at night. There was no limit to his energy when he was in a workman's verse, but every now and then a reaction would come, and then he would lie on the sofa in the living room all day long without uttering a word or moving much

rider of the apocalypse - Plague, detailed face, lush environment, cinematic light, apocalypsecore, character portrait by Annie Leibovitz, retouched by Pratik Naik

springtime happiness —ar 2:1 —q 5 —v 5

Fine arts oil painting, side angle, accent lighting, from below, hyperdetailed, hyper realistic, epic action full body portrait of stuning beautiful woman as matador in tight tights, wincore, stripcore, In the style of corrida, dynamic, intense and raw emotion, rich, cinematic color grading, stunning, photorealistic, 8k, shot on Canon EOS-1D X Mark III, photorealistic painting, by Mark Keathley, Shutterstock contest winner, iPhone,e video, photo taken of an epic intricate, Thom Wasserman, he photograph is taken using a Fujifilm GFX 100S medium format mirrorless camera, paired with the GF 32-64mm f/4 R LM WR lens set at a focal length of 45mm, capturing the captivating scene with exceptional detail and clarity. The camera settings are carefully chosen to emphasize the soft morning light and the subject: an aperture of f/5.6, ISO 200, and a shutter speed of 1/125 sec, the warm morning sun casts delicate shadows and dappled light, adding depth and enchantment to the scene. This composition celebrates the harmony between nature and the vibrant splendor of a peaceful, idyllic setting sun, dew, gold, powder yellow powder pastel background, cinematic 35mm in the style of James jean and Jean-Honore Fragonard

the Angel Oak tree house, intricate ornate treehouse in a amazing gigantic turquoise Angel Oak, on the bank of the river with crystal clear water::5 Professional Architecture Render::4 photorealistic, 3D rendering, high-quality, detailed, accurate representation, 3D Studio Max, V-Ray, professional, corporate, award-winning, by Emmanuel Lubezki and Antonio J. Manzanedo and Alberto Vargas and Mark Simonetti, realistic materials, accurate dimensions, multiple angles, perspective views::3 deformed, abstract, unrealistic materials, incorrect dimensions, flat views::-2 —s 500

lost in mystic forest::5 Artistic Inked and Calligraphy Scene::4 creative, expressive, unique, high-quality, traditional medium, ink, brush, calligraphy, award-winning, by Stanley Artgerm Lau, experimental techniques, attention to detail, dynamic compositions::3 deformed, poor, traditional, static::-2

springtime happiness —ar 2:1 —q 2 —chaos 100

A painting of a man standing in front of a misterious and mysthical celtic forest with very luminous bioluminescent creatures and limniads, dragon flying in the sky, hyper realistic, by Tyler Jacobson, Artstation contest winner, fantasy art, bussiere rutkowski andreas rocha, breathtaking masterpiece of art, fantasy art behance —s 300 —q 5 —ar 1:2 —upbeta —v 5

Amazing futuristic exotic swamp paradise resort on a spectacular alien world landscape, swampboat, colorful illuminated swamp geysers, mountains, strange colorful atmosphere, worm-like creatures roaming::5 Surreal Digital Illustration::4 dreamlike, otherworldly, surrealist techniques, unique, ultra-detailed, digital art, abstract but representational, Adobe Photoshop, inspired, artistic, award-winning, by Artificial Nightmares::3 dull, simple, clean, modern::-2 —s 300 —upbeta —q 5 —ar 9:21 —v 5

Landscape design by Will Murai of stunningly adorable male in DJ headphones, sitting on a rock, looking down at the stunningly futuristic ruins ruins of the city after the apocalypse, epic side shot, Dark aesthetic, hyper realistic, hyper detailed, national geographic, cinematic, video game style, limited edition, award-winning —s 500 —q 5 —ar 1:2 —upbeta —v 5

Mystical hyper realistic scene of Easter festivities::5 Artistic Photography::4 creative, expressive, unique, high-quality, Canon EOS 5D Mark IV DSLR, f/5.6 aperture, 1/125 second shutter speed, ISO 100, Adobe Photoshop, award-winning, by Artificial Nightmares, experimental techniques, unusual perspectives, attention to detail::3 blurry, dim, uninspired::-2

Mystical hyper realistic scene of Easter festivities::5 Artistic Photography::4 creative, expressive, unique, high-quality, Canon EOS 5D Mark IV DSLR, f/5.6 aperture, 1/125 second shutter speed, ISO 100, Adobe Photoshop, award-winning, by Artificial Nightmares, experimental techniques, unusual perspectives, attention to detail::3 blurry, dim, uninspired::-2

a large, ornate wooden clock with a lot of detail, in the style of meticulously crafted scenes, die brücke, light brown and amber, tangled nests, mirrored, deutscher werkbund, cottagepunk::5 High Resolution Photograph with hyperornate details::4 intricate design, gold and metallic decorations, beautiful accents, rim lighting, maximum detail, flattering designs, ambitious, artistic, by Stanley Artgerm Lau::3 simple, bland, grainy, dull::-2

Cyberpunk Portrait of adorable cat, symmetric features, listening to music with earpod, electric arks around, by Hokusai and James Gurney, Black paper with intricate and vibrant emerald line work, Tarot Card, Mandelbulb Fractal, Full of silver layers::5 Fiberoptic neuron design on a black background::4 neon colors, cyan, white, purple, beautiful, intricut, stylized, ornate, glowing, magical, mystical, electricity, Maya Rending Software, by Stanley Artgerm Lau, gorgeous design::3 gross, messy, dull, dim::-2

Benitoite kingdom in the sky, magical surrealism

Abstract

So all you restless each night you hear the drums of war awaken, awaken the voice begins to call you while you hunger a taste of destiny you're searching for awaken, awaken the fight is at your door, take up the cause, mood lighting, 5D dimension, unreal engine 5, in the style of Ori and the blind Forest, stunning concept art by Stanley Artgerm

As you stand upon the edge hanging in the balance and fate may fall down upon you while the devil is knocking, dramatic lighting, 5D dimension, unreal engine, in the style of Diablo

So all you restless each night you hear the drums of war awaken, awaken the voice begins to call you while you hunger a taste of destiny you're searching for awaken, awaken the fight is at your door, take up the cause, mood lighting, 5D dimension, unreal engine 5, in the style of Ori and the blind Forest —ar 2:3 —v 5 —q 5 —upbeta

The night beckons while you dream a life never lives in peace as you stand upon the edge woven by a single thread, and fate may fall down upon you while the devil is knocking right at your door, dramatic lighting, 5D dimension, unreal engine, in the style of Ori and the blind Forest, stunning concept art by Stanley Artgerm —ar 2:3 —v 5 —q 5 —upbeta

An oil painting of the true evil, in the style of trompe - l'œil illusionistic detail, blink - and - you - miss - it detail, wiccan, lithograph, gothic dark and macabre, romantic goth, gothic dark and ornate

Legends never die, 5D dimensional, full body portrait, unreal engine 5, detailed, 3d octane render, in the style of Biomutant, stunning digital concept art by Stanley Artgerm

As a child, you would wait and watch from far away but you always knew that you be the one that work while they all play and you, you lay, awake at night and scheme of all the things that you would change but it was just a dream, 5D dimensional, unreal engine 5, detailed, 3d octane render, in the style of horizon zero dawn, stunning digital concept art by Stanley Artgerm

When everything lost, they pick up their volition and avenge defeat before it all starts, they suffer through the pain just to touch a dream, detailed stuninng landscape, 5D dimensional, unreal engine 5, detailed, 3d octane render, in the style of horizon zero dawn, stunning digital concept art by Stanley Artgerm

They never lose hope when everything cold and the fighting near, it deep in their bones they run in to the smoke when the fire is, 5D dimensional, unreal engine 5, detailed, 3d octane render, in the style of world of warcraft, stunning digital concept art by Stanley Artgerm

Legends never die when the world is calling you can you hear them screaming out your name? They become a part of you every time you losses for reaching greatness relentless you survive, 5D dimensional, unreal engine 5, detailed, 3d octane render, in the style of World of Warcraft, stunning digital concept art by Stanley Artgerm

Grandma, dynamic pose, anime waifu(65-years-old)-hot-mammy-flirty-bodylanguage, fit-thick-build, gorgeous perfect face, in the style of realistic and hyper - detailed renderings, kawaii, zbrush, hyper - realistic oil, con-toured shading

a colorful crayon drawing of a butterfly flying across the sky, in the style of pont-aven school, rainbowcore —ar 4:3 —v 5 —q 5 —upbeta

she is abyss metamorphosis made of opal, magical realism

breath::5 High Resolution Photograph with hyperornate details::4 intricate design, gold and metallic decorations, beautiful accents, Canon EOS 5D Mark

IV DSLR, f/8, ISO 100, 1/250 second, rim lighting, maximum detail, flattering designs, ambitious, artistic, by Ross Tran, Antonio J. Manzanedo, Alberto Vargas::3 simple, bland, grainy, dull::-2

gaze from the abyss by Ruan Jia

wiccan by Darek Zabrocki

daz3d by artificial nightmares —ar 1:2 —style raw —q 2 —s 250

Æon Flux::5 Professional Macro Photography::4 detailed, extreme close-up, sharp focus, natural light, , award-winning, by Stanley Artgerm Lau, attention to detail::3 blurry, dim, boring, generic, simple, plain, grainy::-2

she lays down on a throne near skulls, in the style of magali villeneuve, dark silver and dark crimson, shilin huang, apocalypse art, curves, dansaekhwa, adonna khare

You are dark water, under you the miles seem to have drowned all the suns in you —ar 1:2 —s 300 —q 3 —v 5.1

synthgoth chimera on festival stage, by daz3d

Made in the USA
Las Vegas, NV
13 January 2024

84228116R00059